RATHA'S JOURNEY

A True Story of The American Dream

J.C. LITTLETON

Trilogy Christian Publishers

A Wholly Owned Subsidary of Trinity Broadcasting Network

2442 Michelle Drive

Tustin, CA 92780

For information, address Trilogy Christian Publishing

Rights Department, 2442 Michelle Drive, Tustin, CA 92780.

Trilogy Christian Publishing/ TBN and colophon are trademarks of Trinity Broadcasting Network.

For information about special discounts for bulk purchases, please contact Trilogy Christian Publishing.

Trilogy Disclaimer: The views and content expressed in this book are those of the author and may not necessarily reflect the views and doctrine of Trilogy Christian Publishing or the Trinity Broadcasting Network.

10 9 8 7 6 5 4 3 2 1

Library of Congress Cataloging-in-Publication Data is available.

ISBN 979-8-89333-030-4

ISBN 979-8-89333-031-1

THE VIRTUOUS WIFE

Who can find a virtuous wife?
For her worth is far above rubies.
The heart of her husband safely trusts her;
So he will have no lack of gain.
She does him good and not evil
All the days of her life.
She seeks wool and flax,
And willingly works with her hands.
She is like the merchant ships,
She brings her food from afar.
She also rises while it is yet night,
And provides food for her household,
And a portion for her maidservants.
She considers a field and buys it;
From her profits she plants a vineyard.
She girds herself with strength,
And strengthens her arms.
She perceives that her merchandise is good,
And her lamp does not go out by night...
She extends her hand to the poor,
Yes, she reaches out her hands to the needy.
She is not afraid of snow for her household,
For all her household is clothed with scarlet...
Strength and honor are her clothing;
She shall rejoice in time to come.
She opens her mouth with wisdom,
And on her tongue is the law of kindness.
She watches over the ways of her household,
And does not eat the bread of idleness.
Her children rise up and call her blessed;
Her husband also, and praises her.
Many daughters have done well,
But you excel them all.

Charm is deceitful and beauty is passing,
But a woman who fears the Lord,
She shall be praised.
Give her of the fruit of her hands,
And let her own works praise her in the gates.

Proverbs 31:10–31 (NKJV)

Even though I've read this many times, it never really stood out to me. Like many times reading the Bible, the words went in one ear and out the other. But after I started this book, I came across it again and it spoke—it spoke wonders to me. The more I talked with Ratha, heard her stories, and learned about her life, the louder those verses spoke to me. The similarities between this small woman's life and the biblical virtue of a wife are astounding.

In America, Miss Ratha and her family tried to attend Sunday church service at a local Christian church weekly. She still tries to today, if she feels well enough and has a ride. Yet when asked if she has ever read the Bible before, Miss Ratha's response was "No." You see, she never learned to read in her native country of Lebanon, and after coming to this country as a young teenage mother, she had no formal education on how to read. As most scholars know, ESL, or English as a second language, students do much better with language acquisition when they have a fluent foundation in their home language; this allows them to "transfer" their linguistic knowledge from one language to another more fluidly.

As a matter of fact, she had to teach herself to read but was never able to read fluently in either language. Although she can follow a recipe, read a simple note, letter, or thank you card, she doesn't feel fluent in the English language. The fact that she still struggles with reading can be seen in how she reads her cards and notes; she puts them aside until she has time by herself to decode and comprehend them. Knowing this, it is evident she has not read much of or comprehended much of the Bible, especially with its wordiness full of symbolism, names, old language terms, and history. As a matter of fact, most of us fluent English readers still struggle to comprehend the Bible.

With that being known, reading Proverbs 31:10–31 about a virtuous wife, one can see amazing parallels between this biblical ideal and Ratha's life story. You would think she studied it as a child and spent her life devoting herself to and working towards those ideals or was perhaps even raised in a school of religion where this ideal of a perfect wife was constantly embedded in their heads; the ideal to work towards in life. The similarities between the biblical "virtuous wife" and this small woman you don't know yet, but are about to meet, are uncanny, to say the least.

After escaping the misery of her young life and immigrating to America as an uneducated teenage mother, she was able to achieve the American Dream, alongside her husband and life companion, Fred. This is the amazing story of a woman's life, her story of hardship, perseverance, hard work, and how she achieved the American Dream.

CONTENTS

INTRODUCTION

This is the story of a woman's life, of her survival and success, how she overcame hardships, heartbreaks, and obstacles with grace, respect, and without ever holding a grudge. Her strong core values, along with love, faith, and hard work, enabled her and her husband to live the American Dream.

As a young Lebanese immigrant into the United States at the age of sixteen, Ratha experienced hardships and trials, worked for success, and became somewhat of a legacy in her hometown over the years. Her life is very similar to a Cinderella story. Like Cinderella, this princess was nearly orphaned and was raised by abusive family members. Like Cinderella, she was teased, called names, and had daily chores she had to complete in order to eat or even go to sleep. Like Cinderella, she lived in a big house where she felt unloved, unwanted, and alone. Like Cinderella, her friends were the animals outside in the field (she never had many other childhood friends). Like Cinderella, she had a villainous "stepmother."

But there are also many differences between her life and the Cinderella story. Instead of a stepmother, the torturous villain in Ratha's story was her older, female cousin, Mahalla. Unlike Cinderella, Ratha never had glass slippers or a fairy godmother. She was never made to feel like a princess or ride in a horse-drawn carriage. She never attended a ball, and there was definitely no Prince Charming knocking on her door, although some would say she turned her husband into a prince by the end of their story. Instead of fairy tale magic, this princess had to create her own magic—let's call that "cooking magic." She had to learn this magic, or the art of cooking, by relying on herself, her work ethic, her family, her faith, and her values. And everything she had, she had to earn.

Her faith in who? She calls Him "the Man upstairs." Who is this "Man?" Ratha was raised in a household of Druze—a political and religious sect of Islamic origin, living primarily in Lebanon and Syria. The Druze broke away from the Ismaili Muslims in the eleventh century, and some members of the Muslim community may consider Druze "outcasts." But when Ratha came to this country, she was introduced to Christianity, and now she prays to Jesus. She either attends Sunday services at a Christian church or watches the services on television. Growing up, no one taught her much about religion, faith, or God. Regardless, she claims to have just always known Him, and felt His presence her entire life. If you ask her now, she will say He was there with her "every step of the way."

"How can anyone not believe there is a God? You have to trust in Him. He does so much for you when you trust Him" (Ratha Shabeldeen).

As you read and learn about Miss Ratha, you will soon see how her magic and gifts came to life in the kitchen, how she took the smallest of ingredients and stretched them with flour, wheat germ, salad, or rice to feed her family, even during the hardest times of all. Cooking gave her a purpose, and it was also the way she taught herself how to read: by following recipes. If you visit her today, she is still surrounded by a variety of self-made cookbooks, recipes placed in gallon-sized Ziplock bags or in a three-ring binder, as well as other antiquated recipe books and magazines she refers to—but never quite follows them exactly, as she always adds her own twist to things. Therefore, each chapter is followed by either one of her favorite recipes, one of her most delicious recipes, or a recipe she is known for that tells a good story in and of itself.

My name is Jennifer, and I am an average person. An average person who moved across the country, met the sweetest elderly couple down the street, and fell in love. Truly, I fell in love with this couple, especially her, her genuineness, her strength, her dignity, her work ethic, her love for others, her love for her country, and her love for the Lord. I knew right off the bat, when I first met her and heard her story, it needed to be told.

Someone needed to tell her story so that others, like you, could fall in love with her too.

"It's not a coincidence that she was born on Christmas Day." (Dan Shabeldeen)

CHAPTER 1:
MEET MISS RATHA

Every time someone comes to visit with her, no matter what the occasion or time of day, she insists on serving food—a meal, a piece of some delectable treat she has just baked, or perhaps just a cup of coffee or a glass of soda over ice. Even in her nineties, that is just Miss Ratha. She loves people, and she loves to cook for others. Modern-day folks would say cooking for and serving others would definitely be her love language, as well as her passion, her joy, and a hobby.

But that's just what she does. She has always loved to serve people, and that's probably why she spent so much of her life doing just that—cooking for and serving others. "I just love people!" she says, with her radiant smile and gleaming eyes. "I just love people." Each time she states that, one can genuinely feel the love emanating from this small but powerful woman. After you have spoken with Miss Ratha for a bit, you will hear that phrase often: "I just love people." And every time she speaks it, you are guaranteed she will repeat it again.

But her story isn't all peaches and cream. In her early years, she underwent many traumatic events that some would say should have had devastating results on her. Her mother was taken away from her at a young age, so she was raised without her parents and without love. Instead, she was raised with emotional abuse and sold into an arranged marriage at thirteen years of age, as well as being denied an education.

Ratha Shabeldeen. Born: Ratha Shelbidine, December 25, 1930, in a small rural, mountainous village in Lebanon named Btekhnay. (Her uncle later changed the spelling to Shabeldeen.) Currently, Btekhnay is still a rural town but is also used as a tourist destination for people living in nearby cities such as Beirut and Tripoli. People who come there want to escape the hustle and bustle of big city life. In 2016, the area had only one public school, with approximately four hundred students. Imagine what it was like back in the 1930s!

Both of her parents were Lebanese citizens, but her father had dual citizenship with the United States of America. He served in the United States Army and fought in World War I. Because he went to America to pursue opportunity and earn money for the rest of his father's family, he spent most of his time in the United States. As a matter of fact, he was never even able to meet his only daughter and child, Ratha.

EARLY DAYS IN LEBANON

"We know that suffering produces perseverance; perseverance, character; and character, hope" (Romans 5:3–4).

Ratha's father, Samuel Shelbidine, immigrated from Lebanon to America in 1918 and enlisted in the United States Army. He served during World War I and earned his citizenship. He decided he would take advantage of his citizenship and strive for the opportunity America was just starting to be known for: the American Dream. He was a hard worker and was looking for more opportunity than he had in his home village back in Lebanon. After serving in the United States Army, he had various jobs that included working as a door-to-door salesman selling random household products. Eventually, he was able to open up his own market and purchase some land.

When he got to the point where he wanted a family, he went back to Lebanon to find a wife. After all, cultures didn't mingle back then; it was considered proper for him to marry a Lebanese girl from the village where he was raised. Therefore, he went back to Lebanon in search of a local woman. There, he found a woman who eventually became Ratha's mother. Not long after the marriage, he had to return to America and resume working so he could earn enough money in order to get his new wife her citizenship and arrange for her transportation over to the United States. Additionally, he also had to make money so he could continue supporting his family at the family farm and property according to custom, which required the eldest son to take responsibility for the family after his father passed.

Meanwhile, Ratha's mother moved in and lived with his family. There, she birthed Ratha. The distance for the young couple was stressful, and who knows what her living situation was like there with his family in the house that he owned through his inheritance as the eldest son after his father's passing. Whatever the unfortunate circumstances, the stress turned out to be too much to sustain a long-distance marriage between the two, and they were divorced not long after Ratha's birth, before she was two years old. Imagine being newly married, half of a world apart, literally, with no phones or emails and maybe only a handwritten letter every other month.

Ratha's mom was forced to move out of the house and back with her family in a neighboring Syrian village. Forced to abandon her daughter and be an absentee mom. Unfortunately, Lebanese customs dictated that Ratha had to live with her paternal family. Her mother was literally kicked out of the house and not allowed to have any contact with Ratha, her first and only child (at that time). She was completely banned from the house and surrounding areas and was decisively told never to return.

Afterwards, Ratha was never allowed to see or speak to her mother again or return to her own family in Syria. Ratha recalls playing in the yard and seeing her mother outside the property line, watching her. She knew that was her mother, because she was instructed by her aunt, uncle, and cousins not to look at her, not to wave to her, and definitely not to go over and talk to her. Sometimes they encouraged her to call her mother bad names and use profanity towards her. Ratha wasn't used to speaking unkindly to others, but she would, because she was hoping her father's family might start to like her. Perhaps if she did what they told her to do, they would like her and be nicer to her.

Unfortunately, this never resulted in the effect she was hoping for, as her cousins were always very mean and condescending. Her mother was treated as an outcast and criminal, all because she wanted to visit with and see her daughter grow up. Women, back then, had no legal rights in Lebanon. She was forced to be an absent mother. Ratha can still recall her mother's eyes watching her, yearning to be close to her one and only daughter, even if only from afar.

Her earliest memory is of crying, crying because she wanted her mother. She gives precise details of how her grandmother walked into the room and told her that her mother was gone. Not only was her mother gone, but she was never coming back. Ratha recalls crying more and crying harder, feeling a tremendous pain she had never experienced before. Many years later, she would experience that pain again and learn that it was the pain of a broken heart. Her broken family had caused her broken heart.

"I didn't grow up with my parents, neither of them. So that's why I said my kids will always have a family, with two parents. No matter what."

What a difficult start to life, with neither of her parents involved. Ratha quickly learned she was an unwanted child. However, many girls in the old culture were not valued. Especially to her uncle, who strongly disliked young females and considered them useless—and verbalized this frequently. Most of her cousins didn't like her either. They considered her an unwanted visitor; another mouth to feed; a mouth that would take food off their own plates. Not to mention, teasing and bullying was a common event.

All these factors caused her to feel lonely, sad, and unloved. Every time she cried, her uncle would mock her and say things like, "Oh geez, there she goes again! Look at her cry!" In Lebanon, daughters were not revered like sons were. To many traditional families, they were considered more of an obligation than an asset to be honored. Ratha also had to put up with constant emotional and verbal abuse from her cousins, particularly the girls. They teased and made fun of her constantly, telling her she was stupid, ugly, fat, and lazy. "Look at her! Haha!" is what she remembers hearing from her family members. She never felt the stability of a family unit. She tried living each day to the best of her ability, but living under such conditions, constantly being told she was stupid, bullied and laughed at, left her in tears most of the time.

They even pulled her out of school before she was eight because they stated she was "too stupid to learn." She recalls not only being called stupid, but also being taught to do things the wrong way so that they could later come back and laugh at her. After her uncle pulled her out of school, she spent her days cleaning, caring for her younger cousins, and tending the fields. She was never taught to read or to write because she was denied schooling past the age of eight. Keep in mind that even up to that age, school was an inconsistent occurrence for her with all her other responsibilities.

"They took me out of school because they said I was too stupid to learn. Nothing I did was right. They showed me how to do things the wrong way so they could make fun of me. They wouldn't send me to school; they would keep me at home to babysit my younger cousins. They would say, 'She is too stupid to learn.' So they had me do the farming in the summertime. I busted dirt, planted beans and potatoes, and watered them as they don't have rain in the summer. We had a water pool and had to get the watering can and water the plants. None of them wanted to do it, except me. They thought I was too stupid to read and write, so they kept me busy working. I couldn't learn because I didn't have the opportunity to learn."

Being criticized, bullied, and always set up for failure soon became a daily routine for the young "Cinderella" living with her cousins. At home, she also helped with the family chores, such as taking care of her younger cousins (there were a total of ten children, plus her), as well as working on the family farm. She spent hours and hours outside in the field, breaking up dirt clods behind the plow, planting, weeding, and gardening. Outside was her haven; being alone with the quiet skies and the animals beat the constant teasing and harassment from some of her female cousins inside the house by far. Even her uncle partook in the degrading teasing. She recalls many instances where she was set up to look deceitful and stupid.

"Back on the farm, I would be working. My aunt would tell me to run back to the house and tell her daughter, my cousin Mahalla, to start dinner, so I would. When it was time for dinner and there was nothing to be had, Mahalla would say, 'She never told me!' So I would get the blame and everyone would be mad at me because there was no dinner."

Ratha had a younger male cousin, Lutfi (loot-fey) who loved and adored her. She had patience with him and didn't mind his high energy or inattentiveness. Often times, he would act up and cause trouble for the adults and other children in the house, so he was put in Ratha's care. Ratha tended to him so the adults in the family didn't have to. When it came time to go to school, the two-to four-year-old cousin would follow her. Once in the classroom, the teacher would see Lutfi and say, "Ratha, you can't bring him to school with you. Take him back home until he is old enough to come to school." Ratha walked him home and, by the time she got there, she would realize it was too late to turn around and head back to school. This was what the majority of her "school years" consisted of, until they finally pulled her out for good.

As a child of about five years old, she recalls her cousins seeming to always have money, but she never did. When they all went out into town, her cousins were able to buy things, but she wasn't, for she had no funds. So one day she sneaked into her aunt's room and took fifteen cents, which is approximately one dollar today. Her cousins later found the money, and she admitted that she stole it from their mom/her aunt. At school, the cousins informed the teacher what happened, and that teacher took it upon herself to instill discipline into Ratha and teach her a lesson.

"She took me outside, into the school lavatory and told me to sit on the unfinished floor, which was a cold concrete with hard gravel on it. I had to kneel there for hours, or at least half the school day. I never liked that woman, but she was right. I had done wrong, and I never did steal after that again."

Even family dinners were emotionally painful for Ratha. She recalls all twelve family members sitting around the table, feeling as if they were all staring at her. Whenever she took a bite, they would make derogatory remarks such as, "Look at her eat! See how much she eats? No wonder she is fat!" It got to the point where she didn't feel comfortable eating with them. She felt ashamed, embarrassed, and hated. This is why she had to find alternate times and ways of eating.

With so many people in the family and only one person working to support them (Ratha's father, Sam Shebidine), eating was competitive. Ratha was never able to eat a complete meal without family members commenting on how much she was eating or making other snide remarks. It got to the point where she hated to eat. One afternoon while working outside, she went into the outside room where bread was kept in a barrel. She recalls standing on the brim of the barrel where she took the lid off, leaned down to reach a loaf, and the brim broke. She quickly put the lid back on and ran off to the fields to finish her work and eat her bread in peace.

The next day, the meanest female cousin, Mahalla, asked her if she had broken the barrel. Ratha immediately denied it and acted innocent because she was afraid of the consequences. She then proceeded to question her and ask if she knew who had broken it. Ratha spit out a name—one of her male cousins who lived there and was younger than her. Later that afternoon, she saw the young male cousin tied to a tree, being whipped with a stick by Mahalla. She whipped him so much he had streaks of blood on his body and he cried. Ratha felt so guilty and wanted to confess to save him, but she was too scared of what Mahalla would do to her.

The house they were living in had no inside bathrooms, only an outhouse, often referred to as a "latrine." Living with other females, using the outhouse was competitive—a competition Ratha was usually forced not to succeed in. Whenever one of her cousins saw she was headed to the outhouse, they would try to run there first. Often, they would push her down so they could get there first. Once they made it in, they would sit there and waste time, finally forcing Ratha to go relieve herself in the nearby creek. On her way back from the creek, they would stand there and laugh at her. "Look at her! She's all wet! Betcha she had an accident! Ha! Ha!" But if she made it there first, it was sometimes even worse.

"When Mahalla would see me go to the latrine, she would run in and stop me from going. So I would go into the creek. Mahalla would then laugh at me when she saw me coming in from the creek. If I got to the latrine before her, she would dump buckets of cold water from the creek on top of me while I was inside...this happened for years."

Holidays were even harder. With the close family celebrating, Ratha often felt lonely, like an outsider. Even now in her recollections, she says she always felt like she didn't belong (or perhaps she was just made to feel that way). Her cousins would often complain about her being there; they would complain if she received anything they wanted; and they would complain if she ate too much food or even completed a task better than they did, which might be the reason her cousins often set her up for failure by telling her to do things the wrong way. She was definitely made to feel like an outsider and never felt the comforts of family. Ratha recalls feeling both cheated and socially ostracized during the holidays.

"My dad used to send me money from America, but I never got it. At the holidays, the cousins would all have new dresses, and I would get the hand-me-downs. Often on holidays, we used to go for a walk. We would get in a line and all the girls would get a dime, but I would get a nickel. And it was my daddy's money. I would walk up the hill with them and when we got to the top, they would send me home. They told me they didn't want me with them, and they wouldn't let me go with them."

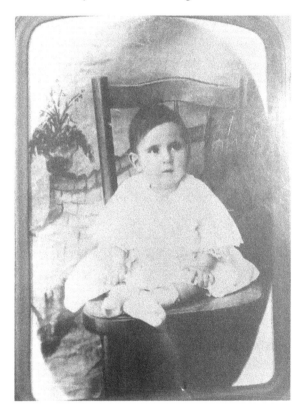

Ratha's dad was the one supporting the whole family back in Lebanon. Not only did he serve in the United States Army during World War I, he also had odd jobs to earn money to send back to Lebanon. This was the only way the family was able to buy things, except for selling or trading some of their farm food locally. As a child, Ratha knew this, which is why it hurt so much that every holiday, the cousins would all get new dresses and suits, and she was stuck with hand-me-downs.

"I was treated like an orphan. My daddy sent money to feed me and help the family, but all I got was hand-me-downs."

Did her dad know how difficult her situation was? Probably not. Communication between Lebanon and America was sparse back then—nearly nonexistent. What little communication there was depended upon ground mail. But her dad was working hard, earning money, and sending it back to the village for the family in Lebanon. He was also trying to arrange for Ratha to come to America, but he had to wait until she was old enough to travel by herself. Ratha was excited and relieved at the thought of leaving her current living situation at the time and coming to join her father in America, where she could finally be connected with a loving biological parent. She could finally be reunited with family. But then, tragedy struck.

When Ratha was twelve years old, her father was living on property and working in a market that he owned and operated in Kentucky. According to the December 7, 1944 edition of Hazard Kentucky's *The Daily Times*, a man walked into the market one evening and shot him, without a cause or reason. According to Ratha, a man walked in and asked for a glass of water. When her father went to get the glass of water for him, the man pulled out a gun and shot him from behind. Little was uncovered about the incident and no rhyme or reason was ever discovered. But, at the young age of twelve, this ended Ratha's dream of finally leaving her tumultuous life in Lebanon and coming to America to meet and live with her father. As one can imagine, Ratha was devastated.

Her father's family was also devastated. Their brother/uncle had just passed tragically and unexpectedly. But this also upset the family's economic situation and survival. You see, Ratha's father had always provided them with money. Not only did he own the house they lived in, he sent them money back from the

States. After his murder, he would no longer be able to send them financial stipends. What would they do? How would they afford to continue living as they were and keep "raising" his daughter (as they saw it)? Since he owned the house and land they were living on, it should rightfully pass on to his only heir, Ratha. That was not that big of a concern, since women didn't and couldn't really own property in Lebanon at that time. But what if she got married? All her assets, all their assets, including their house and land, would pass on to her husband. Everything they had known could soon belong to someone else, and they would be forced to move out and move on.

Was it paranoia, or were the eyes of the young men really on Ratha now? A young, single woman whose assets would ensure a decent and comfortable life; surely many men would be entertaining the idea. The family had to make sure her father's assets remained in the family. So they arranged for her marriage and then told Ratha she would have to marry her cousin.

As you can see, her early years were anything but dreamy. But even today, Ratha holds no grudges. She does still feel the pain as she reminisces and retells the stories, but she prides herself on how much she loves people and how much joy she gets out of being with and caring for others, especially her family.

"I don't dislike any of them, and I don't have any grudges."

RATHA (IN MIDDLE) WITH HER 2 COUSINS

HUMBLE HUMMUS

This is one of Ratha's easy, quick, and tasty go-tos that can be served with her fresh pita bread, on a sandwich, or as a dip with veggies or crackers.

2 cans garbanzo beans
¼ teaspoon baking soda
1–2 cloves garlic, minced (to taste)
½– cup lemon juice (to taste)
2 ½–2 tablespoons tahini

Pour into a pan on stove top, add baking soda and cook 15–20 minutes.

Pour into blender with the rest of the ingredients. Blend in blender until all lumps are gone.

Add more garlic/garlic powder/salt, lemon, or tahini to taste.

Garnish with finely chopped parsley or pomegranate seeds.

CHAPTER 2:
THE ARRANGED MARRIAGE

Ratha's uncle was pressured to decide what to do. The house they were all living in, which once belonged to his father and then to his older brother after the father's passing, now belonged to his brother's only heir: a twelve-year-old female, Ratha. Ratha, a young, naive girl with little education, who could potentially be married off. If that happened, all they had and everything they knew would belong to the man she married, as females at that time in Lebanon didn't and couldn't own property. For sure, "the husband" would take over all the assets and they would lose everything. What should they do? What could they do? Her uncle himself had gone to school but had no work experience; he had no way to take care of the family without the farm the family ran, which would soon be taken away after Ratha got married to a man from another family. The stress and pressure increased. Every day after his brother's death, every day Ratha aged, he worried she would be betrothed to another man outside of the family.

To prevent this from happening, her uncle was pressuring her cousin Farres (Fred) into marrying Ratha. He told Fred that way he could get the money from her father's inheritance. He would also get the house and the farm his family was living on. Additionally, Fred could obtain American citizenship, since Ratha was the daughter of an American citizen and citizenship was also granted to her and her spouse. Obviously, Fred wasn't too keen on the idea, so they warned Fred that there were multiple men in the village who were plotting to kidnap Ratha. Were they using pressure tactics? Obviously. Were they also using fear tactics and bribery? Most definitely. They warned Fred if he didn't marry his first cousin, everything they had, everything they knew, would be taken away and they would be on the streets with nothing. On the streets of a small village, where the economy was based on survival. Eventually, Fred gave in and decided to do what his parents wanted him to. This would not only ensure the family's economic survival and success, but it would also relieve the family of the responsibility of caring for their niece.

Ratha had to be taken to the county offices to file for a marriage certificate. Even though she was thirteen, she was instructed to lie on the application about her birthdate and age; you see, a girl had to be at least fourteen years of age to be married legally at the time. This lie has stuck with Ratha forever, probably because she had to live that lie for the rest of her life. Even today, she still gets her age confused. Probably because from that point on, she had to continue to lie and eventually believed she was fourteen. If you ask her how old she is today, she will jump ahead a year and say a certain age; then correct herself. For example, "I am ninety-three," and after a few seconds of thought, she will correctly annotate, "Well. I'll be ninety-three in December."

"My father's family raised me until I was thirteen. Then, they arranged a marriage with my first cousin, Farres. He didn't want to marry me either, but they told him to marry me, and he would have what my daddy had. So I married when I was fourteen, and had my oldest son Sammy when I was fifteen." (She was actually only thirteen when she got married.)

When asked about her wedding, she doesn't have much to offer. She was so young, it all happened so fast following the murder of her father. She was not only young but naive and in shock. She had to come to the harsh realization that she would never meet her father. That she would never escape her strenuous life situation and escape to America to see her father for the first time in her life, which was what she had been waiting for as long as she could remember. No, that dream would never come to fruition. That dream was squashed, and she had no say in who she would get married to. Like many young females in Lebanese society, she had no voice. They told her everything she was to do, and she listened.

Not only was Ratha in shock and depressed, many of her

family members were as well. Therefore, the wedding was more of a ceremony of necessity rather than a celebration.

"Daddy was just killed, and they were all still grieving—we all were. They didn't want to celebrate and have a big wedding, so they kept it simple. But no one asked me what I wanted; they just told me."

They just told her, all right. They told her what to do, where to be, and what to wear. But no one told her exactly what was happening. No one explained marriage, love, passion, dreams, or even educated her about sex. She truly went into this situation blindly, as most thirteen-year-olds of that time would.

The couple was married inside the house they both lived in. It was a small and simple ceremony and reception, as the family was still mourning the loss of her father, their brother and uncle—an esteemed and respected member of the family and community. They were joined by a few family members and neighbors, but Ratha doesn't remember much more. During that evening of their first night married, she does recall seeing the smirks of her cousins as they peered in the window. She remembers feeling scared and awkward and how she cried. She also recalls the afternoon of the wedding, Mahalla threw her a white towel and smirked as she said, "This is for proof!" It was an awkward evening as the cousins were all trying to peek in, as immature minds may do, which is why most people don't get married inside their family's house. Innocently, Ratha put the towel away the next day because she didn't know what the purpose of it was.

Later on the next afternoon, Mahalla asked her for "evidence." Ratha, again, didn't understand what that meant or make the connection with the white towel. When it was explained to her later on in life, she was absolutely disgusted. Who would do that? Who would ask for such a thing? The thought both appalled and embarrassed her.

During their first several years of marriage, Fred would frequently remind Ratha that he didn't want to marry her; it wasn't his choice. Feeling lowly and unworthy, she would accept his words and look down. It wasn't until years later when she started to find herself in America that she reminded him, "At least you had a choice. No one asked me if I wanted to get married."

"I've known Fred all my life. He was hateful and mean when we were growing up. Back in the old country, the men would always have power/control. But I changed him of that. I turned him into a good man and a good provider for his family."

Ratha and Fred grew up in the same house. While Ratha was breaking up dirt clumps on the family farm and being teased and tormented by her cousins, Fred was at school. At least one of the two had a formal education while growing up; this would come in handy later in their life with their business adventures. For the next year and a half, the couple lived in the same house with Fred's family, as a married couple.

Ratha had her first child at sixteen years old and continued to live with her cousin, now husband, Fred, and his family in their house. Even though she worked on the farm and in the house, she was considered more of a burden than a contributing member of the household. Living in the small village also meant there was little opportunity for either them or for their young child. They had heard stories of other villagers coming to America, known as "the land of opportunity." Ratha had always dreamed of visiting America as a child, escaping her gloom and coming to the land of opportunity, meeting, hugging, and living with her daddy. Although he was no longer alive, perhaps going there would help her feel closer to him. She was already a United States citizen, so making the arrangements wasn't very hard. Everyone they knew that had gone there before them were able to work hard and support their families back in Lebanon. They were able to start new lives away from the desolate village they called home. All the reasons to come to America were staring them in the face. Finally the stars aligned, and they decided to take the adventure, to come to America and seek more opportunity in the new land.

TENACIOUS TABBULLI

An Arabic salad, this flavorful and spicy salad is best eaten with a spoon! Ratha still grows her own mint in her backyard that she uses in this recipe!

⅔ cup burghul #1 (you can use #2 if you can't find, but #1 is better)
2 large bunches of parsley (washed and finely chopped)
1 cup finely chopped fresh mint (or 1/4 cup dried mint)
½ bunch whole green onions, finely chopped
1 or 2 large tomatoes, finely chopped
1 small onion, finely chopped
⅛ teaspoon cinnamon
2–3 teaspoons salt
Pepper to taste
½ cup to ⅔ cup fresh lemon juice
½ cup olive oil

1. Rinse burghul (crushed wheat), drain, then squeeze out excess water. Place in large mixing bowl.

2. Finely chop all vegetables. Add in layers on top of burghul: parsley, mint, onion, green onion, and tomatoes.

3. Add seasonings, mix thoroughly.

4. Just before serving, add olive oil and lemon juice; mix thoroughly.

CHAPTER 3:
THE LAND OF OPPORTUNITY

"After we had a child, we came to America when I was seventeen and my son was eighteen months old. We came on a ship. It was a Marine Corps war ship. The women would sleep on one side of the boat, the men would sleep on the other. We had small soldier beds [cots]. It took twenty-four days to get to America by boat, and it was a rough trip. We got sick on the boat, a lot. All they fed you was hard-boiled eggs and toast. I had to get up to take my son to the top of the deck so he could see the waves and whatever maritime animals were jumping in the water."

Despite their long, uncomfortable travels, the family considered themselves lucky. Lucky to be among the few people who actually got to come to America, let alone come to America as citizens and pursue the American dream. After their nearly month-long journey on a converted war ship, they arrived in New York City and were met by a friend from their village who had previously immigrated to America. He took them out to eat at a restaurant and then back to a hotel to spend the night. They were mesmerized by everything—the noise, the hustle and bustle, the amount of people, the lights...there was so much they had never seen or even imagined before. They had never stayed at a hotel before, or even seen one! They were completely surprised by all the fanciness and newness of this urban life; this was far more extravagant than the little rural village they had grown up in. Probably because of all the excitement and extravagance, they were frightened—too frightened to leave the room.

The next day, the family woke and didn't quite know what to do or where to go. Their eighteen-month-old was hungry, and so were they. Ratha recalls looking out the window and seeing a fruit stand below on the street. Fred ran down, bought three pears, and returned to the room with them. She can't recall ever having a pear that tasted that good. A few hours later, their friend came by to check in on them. They informed him of how they were hungry and had to go buy pears from a fruit stand on the street. He asked them why they didn't go to the restaurant at the hotel...*which is how they first found out some hotels offered food.*

"We couldn't speak English and didn't know how to ask anyone for anything."

They stayed in the big city for two nights. On the third day, the friend took them to the train station, and they traveled to East Tennessee. Their friend had a relative in Kingsport, who had a laundry service with rooms on the second floor. He gave them a room to live in until they learned enough English to get a job elsewhere. Having no education and having to care for their young son, Ratha couldn't work. But Fred did. He worked for a while at the laundry service, and then soon got a job at Coleman's restaurant in a neighboring city as a full-time dishwasher. This paid him $15 a week. Fifteen dollars, for sixteen hours a day, six days a week. That equates to a 96-hour week, for $15, which is $0.16 an hour. With no government programs at all to access, the family had to work hard to survive.

Being in a new country, unable to read, write, or speak the language was difficult for the young family. Ratha had to care for the baby, so Fred was faced with the responsibility of providing for them. This was a huge undertaking that he took very seriously; he did what he had to do to provide for his family. This became not only his immediate goal but also the long-term job he devoted himself to for the rest of his life.

"He was such a good provider. He never told me no. He never told me not to cook for someone or not to get so much at the store. He always made sure we had everything we needed, everything to feed our family and anyone else that would come over; that often meant buying too much."

During her first few months in the new country, Ratha recalls being alone with her young son often. Fred would leave for work and be gone for more than sixteen hours. To pass the time, they would take walks to the park together. If she had some change, they would buy a soda and a candy to split. Ratha needed to do more to help her family but wasn't sure what, or how. After all, she had no education from her home country. Things got desperate sometimes and having only a small amount of money and a son to feed, Ratha needed to make sure she could provide for her growing family, as they had their second child by then. So she began cooking with what was available to her: fresh vegetables, rice, beans, and other inexpensive ingredients. She would take a small amount of meat and use it for seasoning. She became very creative in the kitchen, utilizing the skills she acquired from all that farming in Lebanon to grow small gardens and started making full, delicious meals with whatever she could find.

What was the family expecting when coming to the land of opportunity? While better than in Lebanon, things in America weren't always peaches and cream. There were many emotional, health, financial, and business setbacks that devastated the family, but they knew they had to work through them. Learning the language, learning the culture, learning the transportation system, and trying to meet people and build a support network must have been so exhausting, especially when occurring all at once. Several times, each of them was hospitalized, having been diagnosed with a physical ailment or having to undergo major surgery to the point that some people might just throw in the towel. Some people might just give up, stop working, and go on welfare or disability. Not this couple. When they fell, they always got back up physically, emotionally, and financially.

"I'm the luckiest person in the world to come to the United States. Everything good happened to me here. Back home, I was nothing. People made fun of me. Here, in this country, I was treated like a queen."

AMERICAN BLUEBERRY COFFEECAKE

Almost as American as apple pie! Ratha was ninety when I first met her, and she still had blueberry bushes growing in her backyard. She actively climbed the hill to pick the berries off before the birds did and make as many blueberry delectables as she could!

3 cups unsifted all-purpose flour
1 ½ teaspoons baking powder
¾ teaspoons baking soda
¼ teaspoon salt
¼ cup light brown sugar, packed
1 tablespoon flour
½ teaspoon ground cinnamon
¾ cup butter
1 ½ cups granulated sugar
1 teaspoon vanilla extract
4 eggs
1 cup sour cream
2 cups blueberries, washed
1 cup confectioners' sugar
1 to 2 tablespoons milk

Preheat oven to 350° F.

1. Lightly grease and flour a ten-inch tube pan

2. Sift 3 cups flour with baking soda, powder, and salt. Set aside.

3. In small bowl, mix brown sugar with 1 tablespoon flour and cinnamon; mix well.

4. Use electric mixer to beat butter with granulated sugar, vanilla extract, and eggs, mixing well after the addition of each ingredient

5. At low speed, beat in:

    a) Flour mixture, in 3 segments

    b) Sour cream, in 2 segments

6. Pour ⅓ batter mix into greased pan; spread evenly

7. Top with ½ the blueberries and ½ brown sugar mixture

8. Repeat layering of batter, blueberries, and brown sugar mixture

9. Bake 60 minutes

10. Remove from pan when cooled. Mix confectioners' sugar and milk; drizzle over cake.

CHAPTER 4:
GETTING DOWN TO BUSINESS

"I was at Walmart the other day, and I saw a man standing there with a sign saying he needed money. I walked over to him and said, 'You know, there is a help wanted sign over there. Why don't you go inside and get yourself a job? That's how I did it, I came to this country and worked.'"

If you're looking for financial advice from the Shabeldeens, financial tip number one is: work.

Work, and work hard. As you read about her story and their life together, you will see how hard they had to work. Waking up early, walking and driving through snow and ice, spending hours washing and ironing clothes, living in harsh conditions, staying up late at night, and treating people with respect even when they may not have deserved it. They worked hard to achieve their own business and continued to work hard to run it and support their family and live the "The American Dream."

"I never looked for anything for free. I never wanted anything for free. We went broke three times and I never asked anyone for anything. We worked for it. I washed on the washboard for three years. I had to iron every stitch of clothes, even their socks and underwear, because clothes get so stiff on the drying rack. I didn't mind it; I didn't even think about it."

Financial tip number two is: don't use credit cards.

"If you don't have the money to buy something, don't. That's what Fred taught me. Do not buy things using credit cards or that will put you in debt. If you don't have the money for it, don't buy it." This is in sharp contrast to our modern-day society, where folks get credit and ramp up their debt. The Shabeldeens never used a credit card to purchase things unless they had the cash to pay it right off.

"I learned a lot from him [Fred]. He taught me so much. He taught me how to save money and that if I didn't have the money or cash to buy something, I didn't really need it."

Many of the cousins, family, and friends the Shabeldeens had here were in the restaurant business. Fred's first job in East Tennessee was as a dishwasher at a restaurant. Ratha enjoyed visiting the restaurants because there were always people to talk with and learn the language from, people to teach them about the culture and customs of the area, and people to fellowship and network with. So it seemed only natural that they too would go into the restaurant business.

Fred and Ratha knew the restaurant business from their relatives and tried to venture out on their own several times. The first time, a family "friend" of theirs helped them out. He took nearly $11,000 from the young family—what they received from Sam Shelbidine's inheritance. The friend found them a building and said he would purchase it for them. Fred and Ratha opened a small "restaurant," or more of a pub that served some finger foods, such as hot dogs and hamburgers, as well as bottled alcoholic beverages. Since the state repealed prohibition in 1937, alcohol sales were booming and so was the business, for a short period of time, that is. According to Ratha, the city of Kingsport where the business was located, tried again to repeal liquor and pulled their license to sell alcohol. Without the alcohol, the number of customers declined and so did the profit. Shortly after that, they were notified that their "friend" hadn't actually purchased the building for them. Instead, he put a small deposit down on the building and then took the rest of the money and left town. Even though they were paying him rent, none of the money they gave him was ever applied to the loan. As a result, not only did the business collapse, but they completely lost the money they gave their "friend," as well as all the money they thought they were paying towards rent. The young family had nothing.

"We bought a building from a family 'friend,' who said he

would use the $11,000 we gave him to pay the mortgage and taxes. For two years, we paid him rent, thinking one day the building would be ours. We didn't know; we were young. He ended up not paying on the mortgage and the bank came and took the building over. We lost everything: the $11,000 we put down on it, as well as everything we put into it afterwards."

Not giving up, Fred took other jobs out of state. First, the family moved to New Ellenton, South Carolina and opened up another business. This was also a restaurant, but a drive-through. Initially, the business did well. People loved the quick and delicious meals they could get on the run. Much of their business came from a nearby factory that manufactured ammunition for the United States military during World War II. However, the factory soon closed as the need for ammunition declined after the war, and thus the quantity of customers also declined. This was the second time the Shabeldeens "went broke."

The next job opportunity was in Columbus, Ohio. Fred took a job there as a factory worker. He didn't have the money to take his whole family, so he went by himself. After he got his first paycheck, he sent the money back to his family so they could follow. Despite their perseverance, each place they went to, they experienced more hardships as well as health issues (you read about these hardships in the previous chapter). Things were rough and times were hard for the young family, but Fred did his best to provide for his family and Ratha continued to try to stretch the meals as much as she could with homegrown seasonings, rice, and vegetables.

Fred was working hard, but not getting ahead. Not to mention, they missed the friends they had made while in the East Tennessee area and kept in contact as much as they could. They heard about an Italian gentleman who owned a restaurant on Cumberland Street in downtown Bristol, Tennessee. He and his wife had owned the building for some time and wanted to sell it and retire. Ratha and Fred didn't have enough money to purchase this building or know how to apply for a home loan. But they did know that there was a condominium in Huntsville, Alabama that was in her father's name. So they decided to sell it, and it sold for $4,000. They used this money to pack up and travel back to Tennessee. There, they were able to buy the business (the Bristol Cafe) and rent the two-story building with the restaurant on the bottom and living quarters upstairs. Once back, they got to work and opened another restaurant—their first restaurant in Bristol.

The cafe did well before the Shalbeldeens purchased it, and continued to do well after. It was open for several years and gave the family income, a place to live, people to talk to and learn the language from, and, most importantly, a purpose. They were within walking distance to most everything they needed, and the children were young, so they could easily be taken care of by one of the two adults while the other one tended the restaurant (Ratha always had the early morning shift and Fred would come mid-afternoon and close things up in the evenings). They were saving money on transportation as well as day care. While here, they had two more children, to complete their family of six. But the family was growing and getting older. Their living quarters were becoming tight and the older children wanted to run and stretch their legs outside.

After running the Bristol Cafe for twelve to thirteen years, a local television station (WCYB) made a proposition to the family to buy the building as well as some other surrounding land. They sold the building to the station, which gave them some time to pack and move, as well as enough money to put a large down payment on a modest home nearby. As luck would have it, there was an elderly couple who owned another restaurant down the street from their old business who were interested in selling. Their business was called The Coffee Cup and was located on State Street, across the street from the police station, courthouse, and closer to downtown. So after some conversations and negotiations, The Coffee Cup was sold to the Shelbadeens.

"After we came back to Bristol, we lived upstairs above the restaurant and had two more children there. I saved and saved money and eventually, we were able to buy our first house for $5,500."

Bristol is where they met and hired Miss Virginia Oliver. Virginia was the only constant employee the restaurant had over the years. She was both a waitress and cook who helped in the kitchen. However, over the years she also assumed the role of mother to Ratha and grandmother to her children. She worked hard and always gave good advice, listened patiently, and even kept quiet when the couple would argue, never taking sides. Virginia helped teach Ratha how to read in English, as well as share her recipe books with Ratha, which she had used to help herself learn to read. Virginia was a single woman who lived with her parents down the street from the restaurant in downtown. When her father died, she took care of her mother until her passing as well. When her brother lost his legs in World War II, she also took care of him. Like Ratha, she was always taking care of others and, like Ratha, she was a magician in the kitchen.

The family business became a well-known icon in the city throughout the years. It can be best described as a country restaurant and a place all the locals knew they could go for a good, hot, home-cooked country meal. It was a place for everyone, including prominent members of the community such as attorneys, police officers, salespeople, lawyers, and doctors, as well as travelers and the homeless. It was where everyone knew they could not only get a good meal but also spend some quality time with quality people, including Miss Ratha. Ratha has such a love for people, she would never turn any hungry person away. Customer service was her motto; she believed it was important to respect her customers, and she taught Fred the same. "They're the ones putting food on our table. You smile and show respect." Fred wasn't much of a people person, but she was. The food was always fresh and delicious, and they had repeat customers, especially at breakfast. Some of their most famous dishes included:

- Biscuits and gravy
- Egg sandwiches
- Steak and gravy
- Hot mashed potatoes
- Southern meatloaf
- Baked beans with ham
- Hot roast beef sandwiches (which she describes as an open-faced sandwich, prepared on a roll with mashed potatoes and gravy on it, and of course, coleslaw on the side)

"You don't find food like that anymore. No one has country food like that anymore," comments Miss Ratha.

Although, one could have walked in and ordered just a hamburger, which was equally as delicious as any of her specialty dishes. Especially because the hamburger would be served with French fries made from fresh cut and cooked potatoes the couple harvested themselves in a neighboring plot of land they owned and used for growing fresh vegetables. If the ham in the front window wasn't enough to bring you in, then the delicious variety of fresh cooked country foods would be. And if food didn't tantalize your palate, then a visit with the town's sweetest chef probably would. Everyone knew Miss Ratha and enjoyed her cooking, but her company was equally enjoyable.

"Ratha had everyone coming to eat with her: judges, lawyers, police, and even drunkards," says her now son-in-law John. "They all loved and respected her." She makes sure to emphasize that if they didn't respect her, she had to set them straight so she would earn their respect. She even had a nickname given to her by her customers: "Roxy."

"Roxy" enjoyed her work, enjoyed feeding and serving others, enjoyed providing for her family, as well as conversing with her customers and making them laugh. One cold and breezy fall afternoon, a teenage boy walked into the restaurant and asked Ratha, "Do you have baked beans today?"

Miss Ratha turned around, looked at him sternly and responded, "Did the door open?" It took the boy a moment to get her subtle and sarcastic humor. But then she smiled and said, "Of course we do!"

As mentioned, "Roxy" also believed it was imperative to respect your customers and to teach them to respect you. Often times they would try to put their hands on her, and she would immediately snap, "Oh, no you don't! I don't belong to you" or "Keep your hands off!" And then she returned to her business. The restaurant also served beer and on occasion a customer would have too much to drink and get boisterous. Fred would try to cut them off, telling them they couldn't have any more alcohol, and they needed to leave or walk it off. But the customers liked to argue with Fred. When the arguments started Fred would go into the back to get Ratha so she could take care of business. He would say he didn't know what he was going to do with them— they wouldn't listen to him, were arguing and wouldn't leave. So Ratha would have to go out front and have a talk with them. As soon as they saw her, they would throw their hands up and say, "Oh, okay, Roxy, we'll stop drinking now. If you say so! Call us a cab." As one can see, she was successful in earning the respect of her customers.

Ratha recalls one of her meal items. A typical meal would include one meat item (steak and gravy, chicken, or southern meatloaf), with three vegetable options (French fries and potatoes were the most common), as well as coffee and dessert. This meal sold for thirty-nine cents. Of course, Ratha claims this was back when bread cost ten cents a loaf. Not to mention, these vegetables were always fresh, never canned. One of their investments was to purchase a farm and grow their own vegetables; both Fred and Ratha loved growing vegetables, gardening, and farming. With his hoe and other hand-held tools, Fred would do his share of the farming and harvesting in the morning before coming to the restaurant and Ratha would do her portion of the farming in the afternoons, on her way home, kind of like how you and I now may go to the grocery store to prepare for the next day.

One day while Fred was digging potatoes in the field, a friend pulled over and stopped for a conversation. When leaving, he looked at one of the bushels of potatoes and said to Fred, "I sure wish I had a bushel of fresh potatoes like that!"

Fred handed him a shovel and said, "Here, go get yourself some."

The man replied, "I don't have time."

Fred looked sympathetically at his friend, and responded with, "Well, neither do I. I have to go to the restaurant now and work. You want some potatoes, you can work for them too." So his friend left empty-handed.

The Shabeldeens needed to hire someone to help at the restaurant, so they went to a local employment agency. A few days later, a woman stopped in with paperwork and said, "I was sent here from the employment agency. Can you sign this so I can collect unemployment?"

Ratha looked at her and responded, "Look, I need someone to work here. You want money, you can work here and I'll pay you for it. That's how we made our money—we worked for it. You should too. But no, I'm not signing your paperwork." Ratha goes on to comment on how this country spoils people. "If you are blessed enough to be able to work, you should. You shouldn't just be given money when you are capable of working."

Son John explains how Ratha's presence at the restaurant brought an inviting spirit and joy to the whole establishment and to everyone who came in. She cooked, she collected the money, and she cleaned.

"You kept it all together," he tells his mom. "They all came because of you."

Ratha got to the restaurant anywhere from 4:30 to 5:00 a.m. most mornings. She was there cooking and preparing food. Often times, she was met by people who were sitting outside waiting for her when she got there. She would tell them to come inside, sit at the back table, and get warm while she prepared the gravy for the day's rush of biscuits and gravy. She worked at the restaurant all day, doing all the jobs possible and necessary as well as preparing for the next day. She would usually leave around 4:00 p.m., when Fred would come in to run the business until it closed around 10:00 or 11:00 p.m.

But after Ratha went home, the stream of customers slowed. Was it because most people wanted breakfast and lunch instead of dinner? Was it because Fred wouldn't prepare the meals for them, only warm up what was left from earlier in the day? Was it because folks came to enjoy not only the delicious food but also the lighthearted and uplifting humor and uplifting conversations they could have with Ratha? "When she was gone, they [the customers] would all leave," states former customer John Hamerick.

"Back in the old country, I was nothing. I was treated badly and told that I was nothing. But when I came to America, I left all that behind. I taught myself how to read and how to do things. Whatever I wanted to learn, I did. If you want to learn something bad enough, you can." (Ratha Shabeldeen)

FRED AND RATHA SHABELDEEN

American Dream

Couple from Lebanon makes success through hard work, common sense

BY LAURA J. MONDUL
SPECIAL TO THE BRISTOL HERALD COURIER

Fred Shabeldeen and his wife, Ratha, hold a family photo of themselves with their first son, Sammy, from when they first moved to the U.S. from Lebanon in 1948.

BRISTOL, Tenn. — Seated in their comfortable living room in a pleasant Bristol subdivision, it's hard to believe that Ratha and Fred Shabeldeen came to America in 1948 as a poor couple from Lebanon with little but high hopes, determination and an 18-month-old son.

The American Dream wasn't easy for them. When their boat docked in New York City after leaving their homeland, they didn't speak a word of English.

Ratha, 86, and Fred, 93, grew up together in Burkhaya, Lebanon. As is common in their culture, a marriage was arranged between the two, and they were married when Ratha was 16.

Though she did not receive formal education in her country, Ratha had one thing that helped her young family made it in their

Hometown Stories

ONLINE
View more photos of the Shabeldeens at HeraldCourier.com.

new home — common sense. The family first moved to Kingsport, Tennessee, where they had friends and family. Unable to speak English, Fred got a job as a dishwasher earning $15 a week, working 16 hours a day. The couple then attempted to run their own businesses, one in Kingsport, and later another in South Carolina, but both businesses failed.

"We just didn't understand how

to handle it," Ratha explained. "We couldn't speak the language. People take you for a ride. You think you trust them, and some people can't be trusted."

Finally, the couple moved back to Bristol and opened the Bristol Café, which was on Cumberland Avenue. This time, the business succeeded. They ran the restaurant while raising four children — three sons and a daughter. After 12 years, the building was bought out by WCYB television station, so the

> I couldn't read or write, but I was determined. I made sure my children were all schooled.
>
> – Ratha Shabeldeen

tell them there is no such thing as "I can't." You can do anything you want if you just try. You have to

empty. With her own children grown and moved away, Ratha has become mother to several generations of young people. Neighborhood children come to her house after school, knowing they will receive a warm welcome and something delicious to eat. At 83, she is still spry and feisty, always has something on the stove, and loves taking care of whoever comes by to visit.

In fact, no one ever went hungry around the Shabeldeens. Even

SOUTHERN STYLE MEATLOAF

1 ½ lbs. ground beef
½ cup oatmeal
1 egg
½ cup diced celery
1 can tomato sauce or paste (6–8 oz)

Seasoning:
½ teaspoon salt
½ teaspoon pepper
½ teaspoon garlic salt

Mix all ingredients (except ½ can of tomato sauce). Bake at 350° F for approx. 40 minutes or until done when top is browned. Mix the other half can of tomato paste with ½ cup water; pour over meatloaf. Put back in the oven for another 15–20 minutes.

CHAPTER 5:
HARDSHIPS IN THE
NEW COUNTRY

"Consider it pure joy my brothers and sisters, whenever you face trials of many kinds." (James 1:2)

"He giveth power to the faint; and to them that have no might he increaseth strength." (Isaiah 40:29)

Over the years, the family had to travel to different cities and states to search for new or better opportunities, in order to establish a life for themselves and provide for their children. When one door was closed, they sought others to open. For the most part, they lived on the east coast, including Tennessee and South Carolina, and Ohio.

They started off in Kingsport, Tennessee, where Fred worked washing dishes at a restaurant for very little pay. Then, Fred sought an employment opportunity in Ohio, but didn't have enough money for bus fare for his whole family to travel with him. Therefore, he had to venture out there first, by himself. He traveled to Cleveland and started working at a steel mill factory. After he got a few paychecks under his belt, he sent money back to his family. They packed what little belongings they had, boarded a bus, and traveled to Cleveland, where Fred had established some sort of living arrangements for them. The living situations were questionable at times; many people didn't want to rent to a family with children. Funds were tight and Ratha had to continue to stretch what they had as much as possible. She had to make sure they had enough food to feed their growing family. She became more and more creative with her recipe and cooking ideas.

"Fred worked hard for us. Some people don't appreciate what they have when it's just handed to them. You have to know how to work hard and even struggle a bit to appreciate what you have."

After the family had their second child, they moved to New Ellenton in South Carolina. "It was quite a blooming town with a highway, which most towns didn't have. They built an emission plant, prompting more people to move there. We ran a drive-in, but about two years later, we went broke again. We lost it because we didn't have the business. My husband rode the bus to Cleveland, Ohio and took a job. We didn't have enough money for all of us to ride the bus together. He lived there and we stayed behind. When he got his first check, he sent us money to ride the bus and to rent an apartment—a two-room basement in a house. The woman who owned the house told us not to open the back door because there were big rats that might bite the kids.

"I think I got bit by one of those rats. I was really sick with a sore throat and a locked jaw; I couldn't even drink water. I didn't know what to do. I finally went to a medical clinic, where I stood in line for hours. They gave me a shot of penicillin and then sent a nurse to my house every day to give me more shots of penicillin. I don't remember what they said I had, but they said I could have died. I still had to fix meals for my two kids and my husband during the whole time."

(Rats can have and carry a variety of diseases and illnesses, such as typhus, salmonella, bubonic plague, tetanus, and others. One doesn't have to be bitten by a rat to catch a disease or get sick, but from mere exposure to their bodily fluids like urine, saliva, or feces of an infected rat. Although she doesn't remember what they diagnosed her with, her symptoms are indicative of tetanus, which can be carried in the air and invade a human through a small cut or open wound.)

"It was difficult for us to find a decent place to live with such little money and with children. That was the only place we could afford. We lived there for about a year, but then, many landlords wouldn't rent to people with kids."

While living in Cleveland for a short time, the family went

44

broke again. They completely ran out of groceries and had no food and nothing to cook. Fred had a job but not enough money to buy groceries until he got his next paycheck. So he went to the corner store and found the store manager. He humbly approached the man, and said, "Excuse me. I have a wife and two kids and no groceries to feed them. Can I get an advance on some groceries and pay you back when I get paid?"

The manager looked at Fred and eyed him up and down. Undoubtedly, he noticed the desperation in his voice and eyes, his calloused hands, his neatly ironed but well-worn clothing. He thought for a moment, looked him up and down some more, then said, "You look like an honest and hard-working man. Go get yourself some groceries for you and your family. You can come back and pay me later when you get paid." So Fred did just that. As a matter of fact, he got over twenty dollars worth of groceries, which is almost three hundred today, per consumer price index. When Fred received his next paycheck, he went back to the market to pay the man for the groceries. The manager looked at him and said, "If this happens again, you come over and get yourself some more. Don't let your family go hungry again."

But they never needed to. The family worked hard, lived frugally, and saved enough money to buy train tickets and came back to Bristol, Tennessee, where their streak of luck and success began when they opened the Bristol Cafe.

Fred went back to work at a restaurant in Bristol. Meanwhile, Ratha had been experimenting more and more with her cooking and stretching the meat that they had with vegetables, beans, and Lebanese wheat germ in order to feed her growing family. She had learned to use meat more as a seasoning, less as a main dish, to create delicious meals. Since most of the people they knew from their hometown ran restaurants, and Fred was familiar with working in one, and Ratha enjoyed being in restaurants to talk to people, learn the language, and share recipe ideas, they decided they too would open a restaurant.

There was an Italian man living in Tennessee who owned a building on Cumberland Street in Bristol, and he wanted to sell. It was a two-story building, perfect for a restaurant on the bottom and living quarters above. And it was close to downtown, where people park for work and shopping. So they purchased the two-story building for $4,000.

The family lived there for several years until it was purchased/taken over by the television station that is still there today. Ratha would wake up at 4:00 in the morning, head downstairs, and start cooking. She would run upstairs to feed her children and return downstairs. Fred would stay upstairs with the children until later, since he ran the afternoon and evening shift. They had to hire sitters for their young children, but Ratha still ran up and visited with them as often as she could during the day. Although the Shabeldeens had tried to open and run other businesses in previous years, they were unsuccessful and had to close because they "went broke" as Ratha would say. This new business was called the Bristol Cafe, and it was the Shabeldeen's first successful business.

Financial tip number three is: save money.

Once they sold the cafe to the television station and they moved to their new home, Ratha was happy the family had more space and the children had some yard to run and play in. The house they purchased was about 3–4 miles from the Coffee Cup, and Ratha didn't have a car. So she had to rely on the public transportation that was available to her, such as the bus or a cab. But often times, she chose to walk; this is how she started saving money. Fred would give her money for miscellaneous things, including the bus. But instead of spending it, she would walk and put the money in a jar.

How did you get enough money to purchase a house?

"Fred gave me money for weekly allowance, Christmas presents, holidays, bus fare, and birthdays, and to buy the kids clothes. I would always save some of the money and walk instead of taking the bus. If I had left over money from buying things for the kids, I put it in the jar. Then I learned how much interest was paid on savings accounts, so I opened an account and started putting all the money from my jar into the bank. [She claims a savings account earned 17 percent.] I would walk to the restaurant instead of paying fifteen cents for a bus fare, or more for a cab. After doing this for years and years, I saved quite a bit of money."

The first house they purchased was on Carolina Street in a small, rural town in Tennessee. The family was proud to be home-owners in the land of dreams and opportunity; they were happy to see all their hard work and sacrifice come to fruition. They lived there for about fourteen years and soon started to see the neighborhood toughen up. Some of the neighbors openly used and sold drugs, and Fred and Ratha didn't want their children exposed to that lifestyle. Ratha did what she could to continue to save money to provide more for her family.

So Ratha continued saving her pennies, nickels, and dimes, working hard at the restaurant, and making sure all of her customers were treated respectfully and fairly. Fred did his part by not only managing the business side of the restaurant but also growing and harvesting many of the vegetables they used. These included vegetables like beans, potatoes, tomatoes, corn, and "just a little bit of everything" they used regularly at the restaurant. When the couple had saved a bit of money, they went house shopping again. They found a cute house, but Ratha thought the kitchen was too small. Just next door, there was another house for sale. They looked at the three-bedroom, three-bathroom house, with a large basement downstairs, which was perfect for the children to have their own space. They put in an offer to purchase the house, and that would be their forever house—the house they lived in until after Fred passed and the house Ms. Shabeldeen still lives in today.

When Fred was thirty-nine, he was diagnosed with type

2 diabetes. Because medications for that disease had not been discovered or released at that time, the only treatment was diet and exercise. The doctors warned him of the dangers of diabetes and not taking care of himself. He was informed about the possibility of going blind, having a heart attack or other cardiovascular issues, kidney disease, and having his feet amputated, amongst other side effects of diabetes (also known as the silent killer). For perhaps the first time in his life, Fred was scared. There were several times when he had to be taken to the hospital in the middle of the night because of his diabetes. There were also several times he would have hypoglycemic attacks and start screaming and crying for no reason. This became more and more frequent. Finally, one day Fred announced he would no longer be able to work. He would have to stay home because his diabetes wouldn't allow him to work, and Ratha would have to run the business by herself.

Again, Ratha was not an educated woman. She had hardly any education, nor the ability to read magazines or medical journals well enough to be informed of his disease. Despite all this, she knew better. First, she knew she wasn't capable of cooking, waiting tables, serving, collecting the money, and running the business with all the ordering, supplies, and farming involved. Second, she knew her husband could work. He just had to get it in his mindset that just because he had diabetes, it wasn't the end—only the beginning of a healthier and more regimented lifestyle. So she told him, "You will do no such thing. You will get up, listen to what the doctor said, and go to work."

Ratha spent the rest of their lives cooking more healthy meals and caring for him. Fred ended up listening to his wife and lived a very healthy life with a regimented diet and light exercise, without any complications from the disease until he passed at the ripe young age of ninety-seven.

When Ratha was a child, she faced constant humiliation and criticism from everyone in the family—including her uncle, as well as all her cousins. Fred was on the outside, watching her be criticized and humiliated, sometimes even taking part. Through it all, he too learned to treat Ratha disrespectfully. So is it any wonder that for the first few years of their marriage, he repeated that pattern of emotional abuse and disrespectful behaviors towards her?

"There was a lot that happened, but I am okay with it now. I didn't want to split my family. I didn't want my children to grow up the way I did, without a mother and father. My sister-in-law (also her cousin) called me the other day. Back then, they thought I was stupid. But not now. They all changed their minds. They tell me I have a good reputation in the village we grew up in. My family is the only family from that village that has no divorces. We don't have any divorces. Every other family that immigrated to the United States from our village that we know, every family has a divorce."

Through the years, there was a lot that happened between the two adults, and you will soon read about some of them. A lot of pain and a lot of hardships. There were many days the family had to go hungry and many days they had to go with no heat. There were periods of time the couple would argue and then go weeks without talking, sometimes not seeing one another or even looking at one another, even though they lived and worked together. There was physical abuse as well as emotional abuse. Often times, not talking was the norm for the couple. For Ratha, there were also a lot of trust issues. Events happened that would cause most women to leave their husbands and families, but not Ratha. She stayed. She stayed because she chose to stay, but not without a fight. And that little Lebanese lady less than five feet tall has a lot of fight in her.

Fred was a product of his environment, a Lebanese male who was raised in a patriarchal family that didn't respect women. Instead, women were considered a piece of property. Fred was raised in a house where his own father made constant comments about how much he hated girls—how useless they were and how the world would be a much better place without them. This, even though he had several daughters conceived by his wife. Fred's mother spent her life raising children, working in the fields, and cooking. This male-dominated condescension towards women and patriarchal attitude followed Fred into this country.

He definitely wanted to take control, do things his way, and had an eye for other women. Every Thursday, Ratha would go and get her hair done. After most of these appointments, she would return to the restaurant to close things out and prepare some of the food for the next day. Several afternoons she would return to work and see Fred sitting at one of the back tables with their waitresses, and sometimes even female customers, flirting and laughing.

"I would maybe be gone for an hour or two and when I got back, the restaurant was a mess. Everything was dirty. When I stepped out of that building, everyone else stopped working. I'd have to tell them to get up and get working. I wasn't paying them to sit and socialize with my husband. Of course, Fred was a ladies' man and enjoyed talking with them."

There was one day when Ratha opened the restaurant in the morning and noticed they were missing a whole pot of beans cooked the day before, as well as some ham. The beans and ham were a big seller for the restaurant at the time. Ratha and another cook, Victoria, searched all the places it "should" be until they finally asked the waitress who closed the evening before.

The waitress looked down and tried not to say anything at first. Eventually, she broke down and responded, "Well, you know, last night, the lady down the street called and said she was having a party and needed Fred to bring some food over there. So he took it and left." The lady down the street. Ratha knew exactly which lady that was—one of the shop owners down the street who Fred would frequently visit. He went there almost every day, or whenever he had the chance. But Ratha never said anything because women weren't supposed to stand up to their man, were they? Not according to Lebanese customs back in the old country. A woman should turn her cheek and allow her man to continue with the charade. But then again, Ratha was no ordinary Lebanese lady.

For Ratha, this was it. This was the turning point where she realized she could no longer turn the other cheek. His ways were not conducive to her family; they were quite counterproductive. He was allowing other women to "take food off their family's plate," as she says. The food that would be sold to provide for their family, save for their education, and buy clothes and shoes for their children, he had just given away. For free. Not only was he disrespecting her, he was now also disrespecting her most prized possession and the one thing that held them together: their family. This was the proverbial straw that broke the camel's back.

Ratha went to Fred and said, "I know what you're doing. You need to stop. You're messing around with other women, being a lady's man, and you're taking the food from your own family's mouths. This has to stop. You need to stop seeing her or I'm going to shove her up your [backside]." Yes, she said those words. She hesitated and wanted to replace the "a" word with a nicer word, but was advised by her friend Dot to be honest and real.

"Oh, you're crazy," Fred responded, laughed at her, and walked away.

The next afternoon, Ratha finally went to the office of a local attorney. There, she told the lawyer everything that had been going on. He discussed the steps of the divorce process, completed some paperwork, and took a $50 retainer. When Ratha later told Fred what she had done, he looked at her and said again, "You're crazy. You didn't do that." Ratha directed him down the street to the lawyer's office. There, the lawyer informed Fred of everything she had told him, as well as showed him the divorce papers she had started. He also explained that all Fred had to do was sign the papers, and then he could file the paperwork with the court.

Fred was upset. He was so upset that he stormed out of the office without signing or saying a word, slamming the door behind him. That evening, when Fred got home after work, Ratha had his bags packed for him, ready to go. "You can't keep doing that. You need to change your ways or get out. I'm not putting up with that anymore." He grabbed his bags and left to go to the house of a family friend. He stayed there for a few weeks and returned. Although he never apologized, after that he was a completely changed man.

"I gave him a choice: to either pack up his things and go, or to stop the nonsense he had been pulling. After that, you couldn't have asked for a better man."

Personally, I wonder if he was a little afraid of Ratha after that. Afraid because that "stupid" little cousin he grew up with, who everyone made fun of and looked down upon, was now coming into her own as a developed, independent, and capable woman. Perhaps at this point, he finally saw her as the self-sufficient, hard-working, capable of being independent woman that she grew to be in this country? Perhaps it was at this precise point he realized she wasn't like the passive and docile women in the old country. It took this for him to see that she would call him out on his nonsense. No, she was not like the other women at all, the other women who were reliant on their husbands. Instead, she had become a strong American woman, capable of working, holding together both a business and a family. Providing and caring for her children, loving and nurturing them, as well as providing for the business, working hard, bringing in customers, and standing on her own two feet.

When asked how she got through all these hardships, Ratha looks up and says, "The Man upstairs took care of me the whole time." Then she adds that humor also helped them both along the way. She retells a time when Fred's pajamas started wearing out in the seat of the britches. Fred brought them to Ratha and asked her to fix them.

"Patch it," he said. Ratha knew he really liked the feel of the pajamas and didn't want to spend money on new ones. However, she also knew that there was no way to really repair the worn-out thread in the rear. So she washed them, folded them, and put them back in his drawer.

A while later he went to put them on, saw they weren't repaired, and gave them back to Ratha. "You didn't fix them!" Ratha explained to him that she didn't have any material to repair them with. "Well, find something. Just anything. No one is going to see them when I go to bed anyways."

So that is exactly what Ratha did. She repaired them: she cut one leg off above the knee, and used that material to repair the worn-out seat of his pajama bottoms. She then hemmed the one leg that she shortened, washed them, folded them, and put them back in his drawer. The next evening, he took out the one-legged pajama pants to wear and had a fit. "What did you do to my pajamas?" he screamed angrily.

Ratha chuckled. "Well, I couldn't find a patch to match, so I used the material from the other leg. Now you can wear those pajamas all year. You have one short leg for the summer and one long leg for the winter." At first his face got red with anger, until he realized he had nothing to be angry about and saw the humor in what she had done. He laughed with her and threw them in the trash.

Do you think all these problems made you stronger?

"Yes. It definitely made us stronger. We went broke three times and had fights and hardships. But every time, we learned a lesson and kept trying. We stayed together and made it work. If you really want something bad enough, you can do it."

CURRIED GINGER PUMPKIN SOUP

When things get rough, nothing soothes the mind, soul, and body like a nourishing cup of hot, homemade soup!

1 tablespoon vegetable oil
1 large sweet onion, coarsely chopped
1 large Golden Delicious apple, peeled and coarsely chopped
3 slices (¼ inch) peeled fresh ginger
1 ½ teaspoon curry powder
2 ½ to 3 cups chicken broth
30 oz solid packed pumpkin puree (2 15 oz cans)
1 cup half-and-half
1 teaspoon salt
Black pepper (to taste)

Topping options: roasted and shelled pumpkin seeds or whipping cream

1. In large saucepan over medium heat, heat: apple, onion, ginger, and curry powder. Cook and stir 10 minutes.

2. Add ½ cup broth; cover and simmer 10 minutes (until apple is soft)

3. Pour onion mixture into blender; blend until smooth. Return to saucepan.

4. Add pumpkin puree, 2 cups broth, half-and-half, and salt and pepper. Cook until heated thoroughly, stirring constantly. If too thick, add more broth.

5. Ganish with seeds or whipped cream if desired

CHAPTER 6:
MOTHER AND FATHER

After her parents' divorce at the age of two, Ratha could have no contact whatsoever with her mother. Imagine both perspectives: Ratha, a poor two-year-old who lacked that maternal bond, that essential relationship most of us are able to experience. And her mother, a young woman, her first marriage, her first child, living in a male-dominated society where she had absolutely no rights to her child; her hands were completely tied. She could do nothing. Her child had just been taken away from her like a piece of property. Taken away and prevented from ever seeing or visiting her. The people caring for Ratha hated her mother. When she came to the village to watch her daughter from afar, they had Ratha call her bad names. Ratha was encouraged and told to mock her and make fun of her, her own mother. Ratha didn't know any better. She was so young and just remembers trying to be liked by her cousins and the others in the household who disliked her mother. How devastating and life-altering for both of them.

"When I was young, my mother used to come from Syria to see me, but the family wouldn't let her near me. She would watch me from a distance. She would stand from afar and stare at me. I would see her looking at me, but I wasn't `allowed to go to her. My aunt and uncle used to call me away and talk bad about her, using bad words."

Just imagine her mother's sleepless nights—all the long nights of endless crying. The explosive emotions of sadness, helplessness, and loss. Losing your first-born child, your helpless and innocent daughter. What would become of her? Unbearable.

Although Ratha never really saw her mother after the first couple of years of living with her cousins, she did make contact with her later on in life. After she and Fred were established in the United States, she went back to Lebanon for a visit and contacted her mother. She invited her to stay with her for a few weeks at the Shabeldeen family home, the house she grew up in. Also living in that house were her aunt and uncle, as well as some of her cousins. Ratha doesn't give too many details on the reunion, but she did make contact with her mother and learned about her half-brother, who was born from a following marriage after the divorce. Despite her not commenting much on the reunion, she does remark on her cousins' reactions.

"In 1967, after I was established in America, I went back to Lebanon for a few months and asked my mom to come stay with me. My sister-in-law didn't like it because of the clothes my mother wore. She would wear long veils over her face. My sister-in-law was mean to her and tried to run her off. But I told her, 'If you all had forgotten, you're living in my house. This was my daddy's house and now it's supposed to be mine. So if you don't like us being here, you go [somewhere else].'"

"My cousin never said anything after that. My father had acres and acres in Lebanon, and some other property in another village, and if I had all that property today, I would be a millionaire."

DEANNE, RATHA'S MOTHER AND RATHA

Ratha says her father was actually married six times, but she is his only child. She suspects that every time he was married and went back to the United States, his family spread rumors about his newest bride cheating on him, and he inevitably ended up in another divorce. His plan was to apply for his daughter's citizenship and move her to the new country to be with him. Although he did get her citizenship, he was not able to ever see his only daughter migrate to the new country and start her new life. Unfortunately for both of them, the day when he got to see his only daughter come to America never came.

Her father, Sam Shelbidine, had settled in Hazard, Kentucky after serving in the United States Army. He spent several years as a door-to door-salesman and then opened and operated a convenience or liquor store in Hazard. According to Ratha, he was working there one evening when a man came in and asked for some water. He turned around to get it and was shot and killed from behind. The newspaper cites only that he was "fatally shot Tuesday night, in his liquor store in Hazard, allegedly by a bandit who ransacked his cash register and escaped with bills" (*The Daily Times*, Hazard Kentucky, December 7, 1944). Less than two months before turning fourteen years old, Ratha's dream of meeting her father came crashing to an end.

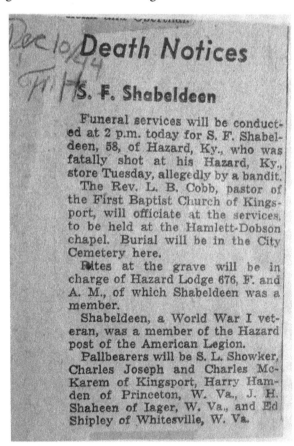

Death Notices

S. F. Shabeldeen

Funeral services will be conducted at 2 p.m. today for S. F. Shabeldeen, 58, of Hazard, Ky., who was fatally shot at his Hazard, Ky., store Tuesday, allegedly by a bandit.

The Rev. L. B. Cobb, pastor of the First Baptist Church of Kingsport, will officiate at the services, to be held at the Hamlett-Dobson chapel. Burial will be in the City Cemetery here.

Rites at the grave will be in charge of Hazard Lodge 676, F. and A. M., of which Shabeldeen was a member.

Shabeldeen, a World War I veteran, was a member of the Hazard post of the American Legion.

Pallbearers will be S. L. Showker, Charles Joseph and Charles Mc-Karem of Kingsport, Harry Hamden of Princeton, W. Va., J. H. Shaheen of Iager, W. Va., and Ed Shipley of Whitesville, W. Va.

Murder Victim To Be Buried In City Sunday

Funeral services for Sam Shelbidine, 58, native of Syria, resident of Hazard, Ky., for the last 15 years, will be conducted Sunday at 2 p. m. at the Hamlett-Dobson Chapel. Burial will follow in the City Cemetery. The Masons will have charge of the service at the grave.

Shelbidine was fatally shot Tuesday night in his liquor store in Hazard, allegedly by a bandit, who ransacked his cash register and escaped with bills. Search for the slayer is being made through eastern Kentucky and one suspect is being held at Winchester, according to the Kentucky State Highway Patrol.

Friends of Shelbidine have posted a $500 reward at the People's Bank, at Hazard, for information leading to the arrest of the slayer.

Shelbidine is survived by a daughter, a sister and brother in Syria, a cousin in Kingsport, and other cousins of the surrounding territory.

The body came to Kingsport from Hazard Thursday and remains at the Hamlett-Dobson Funeral Home.

Death Notices

Not being able to ever meet her father or have a relationship with him is her biggest regret in life, as if she had anything to do with that. But what makes it even more painful is *why*? She never knew why her father was shot and murdered. Why did some random person come into the store and kill her father, who was a genuinely nice person and liked by all who knew him?

"My daddy was loved by everybody. Everybody who met him told me what a good and honest man he was. I wish I knew him."

Not only did she have to live with the fact that her father was murdered and that she never did or will meet him, but she also didn't know why. Was there a reason? Was it really just for money or was it something else? Was it a random act of violence or was it a plotted incident? Was it a hate crime? Not knowing her father and never being able to meet him was probably one of the biggest heartbreaks of her young life; the second time she experienced that sharp pain she now recognizes as a broken heart.

$500 REWARD

For information resulting in the arrest of the person

or persons who murdered Sam Shelbidine.

The money is on deposit in the Peoples Bank and

in the custody of F. L. Cisco.

Guaranteed by

I. M. BROFFITT

When Ratha's father died in 1944, her uncle panicked. What would happen to the house that they were living in (in Lebanon)? What would happen to all the other property he owned? Her uncle had never worked; he spent his life "taking care of" the women and children while his brother, Sam Shelbidine, came to America to work and send money back to the family. Having no means to support himself, his family, or his brother's daughter he had been caring for, he decided to forge his brother's will. According to Ratha, he contacted the Kentucky state government and claimed that her father left most everything to him, or at least most of his monetary assets and the property he had purchased in America. Don't forget, this was in addition to the house, farm, and property he had in Lebanon. At that time, it was almost a half million dollars. For as long as Ratha could remember, her uncle had lived off of and supported his family with the money her dad sent to them After her father was killed, her uncle was able to continue living off of his inheritance, which fueled the fire of preventing Ratha from marrying outside the family.

Ratha is very aware that if she had that land today, she would be a millionaire. But she isn't upset or angry about any of this. She just sees this as the way things happened. She doesn't count how she was wronged or scorned; she counts her blessings. She takes pride in her work, in all she and Fred were able to accomplish in this country, and most importantly, in her family. She is proud of her family, proud of the discipline she and Fred used to get where they did, proud of the sacrifices they made for their family and business, and proud of all the long hours and hard work they put in to make their dreams come true.

LOVE THEM LEMON BARS

Crust:
1 cup (two sticks) unsalted butter
½ cup granulated sugar
2 cups flour
⅛ teaspoon salt

Filling:
6 extra large eggs (at room temp)
3 cups granulated sugar
2 tablespoons grated lemon zest (from 4–5 lemons)
1 cup freshly squeezed lemon juice
1 cup flour
Powdered sugar for sprinkling on top after baking

1. Preheat oven to 350° F.

2. Prepare crust: cream butter and ½ cup sugar until light and fluffy.

3. Add flour and salt; use mixer to add to butter mixture.

4. Place onto a board, gather into a ball. Flatten dough with floured hands and press into a 13 x 9 inch baking sheet with ½ inch edge all around. Put into refrigerator for at least 30 minutes.

5. Bake for 15 minutes; let cool on wire rack.

Filling:
Whisk all remaining ingredients until thoroughly mixed and fluffy.

Pour over crust and bake for 30–35 minutes, until filling is set. Let cool; sprinkle with powdered sugar.

CHAPTER 7:
BREAKFAST FOR EVERYONE

"I've never let a hungry person go hungry. I fed every single one of them that came" (Ratha Shabeldeen).

"For I was hungry, and you gave me food. I was thirsty and you gave me drink. I was a stranger and you welcomed me." (Matthew 25:35)

After years of living in poverty and making the most of what they had, Ratha loved being able to provide for her own family. She had always worked on the farm and was familiar with many of the fresh vegetables, herbs, and spices used in food. When in America, she was forced to make a small amount of food stretch into a meal. The fact that she could also cook and provide for others became a passion. So how does a young woman, who was never taught to read or write in her native language, come to this country and learn to read and write in English? (She claims not to be able to read or write very well, but she can sure follow recipe directions and write some of her own!) Basically, she taught herself.

The first cook at the restaurant was Miss Ratha herself. However, with increasing numbers of patrons and a growing family, she soon realized she needed some help. The first hired cook was Virginia Oliver. She was initially hired as a waitress, and quickly learned everything she could about cooking and the restaurant business. Eventually, she helped with the cooking as well. She was a trusted employee and close friend to Ratha. She had no children of her own, but assisted with the raising of Ratha's children and truly became a grandmother to them. She was definitely like a mother to Ratha; she helped teach Ratha how to read and write in English. Virginia used to get magazines that Ratha developed an interest in; she wanted to use them to learn how to read, particularly the recipes. Ratha would ask Virginia if she could have the old magazines when she was done with them. Initially, she laughed at Ratha, joking, "What are you going to do with those? You can't even read." Well, Ratha wanted to learn to read. This comment fueled her desire to read even more. She recalls proudly tucking them under her arm and taking them home with her. "I took them home and everywhere I went. I took them to the restaurant, to bed; whenever I had a few moments to read, I had the magazines with me to practice. When I came across unfamiliar words, Virginia would explain to me how to pronounce and how to understand them." Learning to read was difficult, but Ratha was determined to learn. Her response was simple, "That's exactly what I am going to do with it—learn to read." And so she did. She taught herself how to read, how to follow new recipes and become a better and better chef.

She learned to read well enough to get by and open and operate two successful restaurant businesses. While she learned to cook a variety of foods and meals, breakfast was probably her favorite meal to serve.

Ratha recalls two of her small-town restaurants, Bristol Cafe and the Coffee Cup, both located in downtown Bristol, Virginia. "If I had a penny for every egg I cooked, I'd be a rich woman today!" She has said this multiple times, usually after preparing a delicious egg sandwich on homemade pita bread. Ratha loves to cook. She also loves being able to provide for her family and for others. She loves to make people happy; she loves to hear them chatter, converse, and laugh. She also loves to share with and help others, and commonly states, "If God gives it to me, I'll share it with others who need it." And sharing with others in need is just what she did. She reminisces about how the homeless would line up outside her doorstep when she first entered the restaurant at 5:30 a.m. They were there because they were cold, they were hungry, and they were grateful to have a place they could come.

When she opened the restaurant in the early winter mornings, close to the Appalachian Mountains, temperatures would be near or below freezing at times. The icicles would form off the eves outside and there was no place to seek shelter during the long and cold nights. The homeless knew she would be opening the restaurant soon. So they came and sat close to the front door, where she would open it and say, "Go sit down at that table over there and get warm. I am going to go make biscuits and gravy in the back."

Sometimes she would come out with a dime and ask them to go get a newspaper for her. When she did, all of them would jump up and offer to be the one to go get it for her. She had to settle the "debate" by saying, "You can go tomorrow." When she was done preparing the meals, she would serve them. She never charged them because she knew they didn't have any money but needed a hot meal.

And that's exactly what she would do. Make biscuits and gravy to feed the homeless and hungry. "God gives it to me so I can share with others who don't have it." But Ratha was no fool; there were many folks through the years that tried to skip their bill. She treated these folks differently because they could afford it. According to Ratha, if you could afford your meal, she expected payment. And yes, she could always tell the difference between a needy person and a greedy person. The needy ones had a full but desperate heart; the greedy ones were selfish and were looking for handouts. Miss Ratha was able to tell the difference. She loves people and is able to see their true hearts.

"I loved making breakfast for others," she says with a smile on her face and a gleam in her eyes. She then begins to tell the story of a man that came in to the restaurant one morning, telling her his story. He was a hitchhiker who was traveling through town and had no money or funds. The evening before, he tried to get a room at the Salvation Army, but there were none, so he walked to a nearby church where he was able to cuddle with a bush and rest for a few hours.

When Ratha opened the restaurant at 5:30 a.m., this young

man came by, happy to see lights and a warm place to sit for a while and maybe be lucky enough to grab a bite to eat. (Some of the locals had recommended he go see her). Or perhaps just sit in a warm place and defrost, at least until the sun came up. Ratha didn't recognize him as she did many of the other regulars, but she could tell he was a passerby, someone traveling through the area on foot. He was hungry and explained what had happened to him the night before and how he had to spend the night sheltered by a nearby bush. It was obvious to Ratha he was hungry, he was cold, and he was in need. So Ratha did what she always does for others in need—she gave him a hot breakfast. She still recalls exactly what it was: two eggs, bread/toast, bacon with some gravy, and a cup of coffee. After he ate, he thanked her and left. Ratha never saw him at her door in the early morning again.

The next summer, a man she didn't recognize came into the restaurant and walked straight up to Ratha. He looked her dead in the eyes and said, "Do you remember me?" She looked at him and didn't quite remember who he was, and shook her head no. "I was here last fall and you gave me breakfast when I was stranded, cold, and hungry. I am here to pay you for it."

It took Ratha a few moments to remember exactly who he was, but she eventually did. Instead of taking any money, she refused it. "Look, if I gave you something, I gave it to you. I'm not taking it back now by taking money from you." He tried to insist and hand the money to her, but she continued to refuse. Undoubtedly, he soon realized he couldn't bend this strong-willed woman's will. They finally reached a compromise when Ratha said, "Look, if you're hungry this morning, I'll give you breakfast again. But this time, you can pay me for it." So it was settled. He ate another one of Ratha's fabulous breakfasts and this time, Ratha accepted payment for it.

"I never let anyone go hungry. There's a lot of people who I didn't give anything because they tried to sneak a free meal. I can tell the people who really need it. If they don't need it, they had to pay for it. They had to work for it, just like I did. I made my life that way, by working for it."

"I enjoy doing it. I just love to do what God tells me to do. Share with people. God gives it to you, and you share it with others."

Without a doubt, Ratha believes in God and that He watches over her because she trusts and has faith in Him. She tells of a car accident she had one early winter morning on the way to the restaurant to prepare breakfast. The roads were full of ice and she was driving cautiously down the road when her car slid towards a cinder block wall. She crashed into the wall, breaking apart the blocks, then bounced and spun around towards the other side of the street, where she went down an embankment and into a wooded area full of trees. She states she gave up and exclaimed, "Jesus, help me." Her car navigated through the trees in the wooded area and stopped.

She sat there for a bit, in shock, until two men knocked on her car window. They got her out and assisted her. The police were called, and they arrived at the scene to make an accident report. Everyone was amazed that Ratha was standing, walking, without even a scratch on her face. Her car was demolished, but she was fine. After she called Fred and informed him of the accident, the police officer offered to drive her home; but Ratha refused. "No, I want to go to the restaurant. I have to get breakfast ready."

Several weeks later, she went to a gas station close to where she slid off the road. The station attendant asked her, "Are you Miss Shabeldeen? Aren't you the one who crashed into the wall and then into the woods?" She shook her head yes.

"How did you do it? How did you survive?"

Ratha looked at him and had the answer before he even finished his question. "It wasn't me that was driving, that's for sure. It was the man upstairs," she said as she smiled, looked up towards the sky, and put her hand over her heart.

FRIED EGG SANDWICH

If you've ever been to Ratha's house in the morning, undoubtedly you were or would be offered a fried egg sandwich. "If I had a penny for every egg I cooked, I'd be rich," Ratha says.

Egg(s)
Pita bread
Lettuce
Tomato, sliced
Mayo, to taste
Salt and pepper to taste
Fry the egg sunny side up in a pan; season to taste.
Put the egg on pita bread.
Ratha adds mayo, freshly sliced tomato, and lettuce.

HUMBLE HASHBROWNS

A lawyer working down the street from the Shabeldeen's restaurant the Coffee Cup often visited for breakfast. He especially loved the hashbrowns and asked Ratha for the recipe one day. Ratha told him how to prepare them. (It's quite simple, as you can see.) He went home and tried preparing them for his wife. He returned several days later, very disappointed, and told Ratha that his wife, Jan, wouldn't even try them.

"What did you do?" Ratha asked. When he explained his process to Ratha, he included that he "shredded" the potatoes and onions in the blender, with a small amount of bacon grease. It turned out to be more of a mushy pancake soup rather than hashbrowns. Ratha loves retelling this story and laughs every single time.

REMINDER: DO NOT use a blender to "shred" your potatoes or onions.

2–3 potatoes, washed, peeled, and shredded
Salt (to taste)
Dash of pepper (to taste)
¼ cup shredded onions
Bacon grease (to cook in; tastes better)
Shred potato and onion; drain excess water.

Put in a skillet with a little bacon grease (or butter, but bacon grease makes them taste better). Form one handful at a time, spread and flatten in a pan. Salt, then cook until golden brown on each side (like a pancake).

CHAPTER 8:
PEOPLE

"Beloved, let us love one another, for love is from God, and whoever loves has been born of God and knows God" (1 John 4:7).

"I just love people!" Ratha will say repeatedly, with a gleaming smile. You can just feel the love emanating from her genuineness.

Miss Ratha made a life out of talking to, cooking for, serving, and loving on people. Anyone who met her and had a brief conversation with her would love her. Anyone who did something kind for her or the Shabeldeen family would undoubtedly be repaid by receiving a meal, a ham, or some bundle of treats to show her appreciation and her love. Because she loves people so much, there needed to be an entire chapter written with just that title.

"People are your friends. They are like food—you can't live without them."

She starts talking about random people she has met at the grocery store, at the library, and other various places around town who recognize her and say hello. At the grocery store one day, there were two women who were whispering behind her, calling her "the pie lady." When she heard, she smiled, turned around, and asked them if they were talking about her. "It is you!" they exclaimed with excitement. They told her stories of how they remembered her from the bakery and loved going in to get her pies. Sometimes she doesn't even remember who they are or how she knows them. But living in a small town, working in and running a restaurant most of her adult life, she knows a lot of people. Some folks remember her from the restaurant, but now that she is in her nineties, most customers have either passed or don't go out in town very much. She also knows others who she worked with either at the bakery or high school following her retirement from the restautant business. Basically, wherever she goes, she is like a celebrity, with people running up to her, giving her hugs, and starting conversations with smiles and happy memories.

There are many adjectives you could use to describe this woman. Many have been mentioned in previous chapters, but one word that definitely stands out is *feisty*. Yes, she is a high spirited, happy, and feisty lady. Even in her nineties, she will definitely keep you on your toes!

"I don't get mad at people; I do like messing with them. And when I do, I'm having fun. I am enjoying life. Sometimes you got to mess with people to have fun."

One afternoon Ratha was working in the restaurant when a man came in and ordered a beer. At that time, a beer was one dollar, so he gave her a five-dollar bill and she gave him change. He took one of the dollar bills and threw it in Ratha's direction and said, "Here, buy yourself a beer." Ratha responded, "No thanks, I don't drink beer," and she slid the dollar bill back to him on the table.

The man was astounded, sat back, looked at her sternly and replied, "You don't? How do you work at a place like this and not drink beer?"

Ratha stated, "That's because my husband told me beer is for selling and making money, not for drinking." She laughed and walked off, leaving the customer to ponder his existence at the counter with just a beer.

Even in her nineties, she is spirited and feisty. She constantly cracks subtle jokes that you might just miss if you're not paying attention.

While she was working at the restaurant one day, a man came in with his young son, who was probably around eight years old. The man explained he was there so his son could learn how French fries were made, and he was hoping Ratha would let him watch her. So she grabbed the potatoes she had already peeled and had soaking in a bin of water and started slicing the potatoes up. She threw them in a fryer with vegetable oil and added onions and salt. The young boy watched with big eyes, amazed at what he was seeing. "What's she doing, Daddy?" the young boy asked his father. The dad had to remind him that she was making French fries. The young boy's face got brighter and he asked Ratha, "So that's how you make French fries?"

Ratha nodded yes and asked if he had ever eaten them before.

"Yes," the boy responded, "but I thought they came from a bag in the freezer."

Most of her kids ate every single meal at home. They and their friends would come over and sit in the kitchen while she cooked and laughed with them. Even when she offered to get them something to eat away from home, her sons would say, "Is it too much trouble if you just cook us something?" And of course, this amazing woman and mother would smile (well, maybe not smile on the outside, but cooking for others and having them at home with her made her smile on the inside) and respond, "Of course I can." And just like that, sometimes in a matter of minutes, an amazing meal would be served.

Even today, long after retirement (twice) and in her nineties, Miss Ratha still has people over almost every day, visiting, chatting, bringing a gift, and partaking in a meal or dessert of some sort. (Even if you're not hungry, you will eat.) Like many people, she dislikes being alone, and the passing of her husband, Fred, hit her hard.

PUMPKIN CHEESECAKE

Crust:
¾ cup graham cracker crumbs
¼ cup granulated sugar
½ cup butter, melted

Pie:
8 oz cream cheese, softened
2 eggs, beaten
¾ cup sugar
2 cups canned (or cooked and mashed) pumpkin
1 package instant vanilla pudding mix
¾ cup milk
⅓ teaspoon ground cinnamon
Dash of nutmeg
12 oz/1 container thawed whipped topping, divided

1. Preheat oven to 350° F.

2. Mix graham cracker crumbs, ¼ cup sugar, and melted butter in bowl. Mix until blended and press into the bottom of a 9-inch springform pan.

3. In a separate bowl, beat cream cheese, eggs, and ¾ cup sugar at medium speed for 2 minutes, or until light and fluffy.

4. Pour into pie crust.

5. Bake approx. 30 minutes, until done and batter is firm (use stick test). Remove to a wire rack to cool completely.

6. Beat remaining ingredients (pudding mix, pumpkin, milk, whipped topping, and seasonings) with electric mixer then spread over pie. You can decorate with dollops of whipped cream or more cinnamon.

7. Immediately refrigerate.

CHAPTER 9:
SWEET REVENGE AND
LESSONS LEARNED

"Do not seek revenge or bear a grudge against anyone among your people, but love your neighbor as yourself" (Leviticus 18:19).

In Genesis, we can read about Joseph and how he was betrayed by his brothers. Not only did they plot against him, but they also considered murdering him. They ended up selling him into slavery for a profit. Undoubtedly, Joseph was hurt and traumatized by their mistreatment and abandonment. We also read that he became a high-ranking Egyptian official, second to the pharaoh himself:

"Then Pharaoh said to Joseph, 'In as much as God has shown you all this, there is no one as discerning and wise as you. You shall be over my house and all my people shall be ruled according to your word; only in regard to the throne will I be greater than you'" (Genesis 41:39–40).

Years later and second in command to the pharaoh, Joseph met his brothers again, face to face. Shouldn't Joseph have been vindictive and vengeful towards his brothers? One would think. But instead, he acted more godly towards his brothers. He saw how God's hand was at work through it all and he was able to secure land and food to allow people to survive through a long famine. He was able to forgive his brothers, love his brothers, provide for his brothers, and reunite with them.

Joseph told his brothers, "God has made me Lord of all Egypt. Come down to me, do not tarry. You shall dwell in the land of Goshen, and you shall be near to me" (Genesis 45:9–10).

This is so similar to Ratha's story. After escaping the misery of her youth where she was verbally battered, told she was stupid and didn't know anything, and forced into an arranged marriage so her property could be taken from her and besieged by her uncle's family, she would once again face her family members who emotionally abused her, betrayed her and, like Joseph's brothers, sold her for a profit.

Ratha may not have been "sold" into slavery, but she was sold into a marriage. An unwanted, arranged marriage. A marriage where they profited by receiving land and money. Not to mention that in the house in which she was raised, she was more of a servant than a family member. She was teased and neglected, denied an education, and told she was stupid and fat. She was forced to clean, farm, and care for her younger cousins while wearing torn and tattered hand-me-downs. Like Joseph, she would one day see her oppressors again—her aunt and uncle—face-to-face. Like Joseph's brothers didn't recognize him when they saw him, her family wouldn't recognize her either. After leaving and breaking the chains of oppression, she came to America to live her best life by working hard. How would she react when she had to face her oppressors?

Sometime in the 1980s, Fred's parents came to America to visit with the family. They stayed with Fred and Ratha for six months. They got to meet their grandchildren, spend time with them, visit with their son and see the family-run business for themselves. They got to see Ratha run a household and a business. They got to taste her cooking, meet some of their frequent customers, and get a view of the life they had established for themselves in America. Ratha greeted them with excitement, love, and grace. During this time, Ratha enjoyed showing them everything she had, everything she had learned, and everything they had accomplished as a family from hard work. She enjoyed preparing meals for them, taking them shopping, and getting to know them on a new level—a personal level.

"I enjoyed every minute of it. It was so much fun when they were here. I treated them better than if they were my own parents."

Not only did Ratha house them for all those months, cook

for them and supply them with their necessities, she also took them shopping at local department stores. This was quite a treat for them, since they weren't used to big department stores in their small village. If you wanted new clothes, you would have to see a "dressmaker." Ratha treated them to things like sweaters, perfumes, and shoes. Her mother-in-law's eyes were as big as a child's in a candy store for the very first time. All the selections, varieties, and colors of apparel and accessory items available enthralled her. There were many situations where she couldn't decide which one to buy. The only thing Ratha could think of doing was to buy both of them for her.

"I wanted her to have them. I treated her just like she was my own mother. I wanted her to be proud of me and feel loved."

She treated her father-in-law the same way, buying him things from the department stores without him asking, cooking his favorite foods, and driving them around to sightsee and spend time with the grandchildren at their different events. I was never able to talk to Fred's parents about their stay, but if their eyes lit half as much as Ratha's do when she talks about their visit, it would be safe to say they had a fabulous time visiting them and seeing their success in the new land.

At the end of the six-month visit, the couple returned to Lebanon. They shared with their small village all about the couple's family, their success, the business, and the grandchildren, as well as the unforgettable memories and good times. They shared Ratha's significance in raising the children, holding the family together, her amazing cooking, her work ethic and entrepreneurship. Who would have thought the young girl they called "too stupid to go to school" would teach herself how to read, would grow into a successful mother of four kids, hold her household together, and run a business, as well as be a prominent member in the community? This was the time that perhaps "freed" Ratha from all the negative memories of her childhood. Instead of being that "stupid" girl that always did things the wrong way, they were able to see her as a successful wife, mother, and businesswoman. This made Ratha feel a tremendous sense of redemption and accomplishment.

"[Fred's father] never acknowledged me as his niece when I was a child, nor as a daughter-in-law later on. It wasn't until I took him here to this country and showed him who I really am... When they came back to Lebanon, they told everyone about me and built up my reputation. They told people there that if it wasn't for me, their son would have nothing."

Despite all the adversities she experienced as a child, Ratha never got angry or set out for vengeance of any sort. Rather, she was thankful for the lessons learned and all the blessings she had been granted from "the Man upstairs," too much to focus on negativity of any sort. Instead, she loved. She loved them wholeheartedly.

Because Ratha had learned early on not to take what wasn't hers, people respected her and considered her to be a good steward with money.

Years later when Ratha owned and operated her restaurant, people would sometimes come into the restaurant with large amounts of money. They would say they were going to go have a night on the town, and would ask to leave a large sum of money with her so they didn't spend it. "We're going to go have a good time. Please, watch this for us so we don't spend it all."

They would then go out, have fun, and forget about leaving the money with her. Weeks later they would come back into the restaurant and complain that they were short of money and needed to pay rent. She would then say, "Don't you remember? You left that money with me."

"They would always respond, 'Did I really??!' Every time. They forgot they even left money with me!"

"Sometimes I thought of using that money, but then I would think about what happened to me when I was younger—of kneeling on the dirt and gravel floor at school for half a day for stealing fifteen cents. I never stole again. Ever."

TO DIE FOR PUMPKIN PIE

If you like pumpkin pie, you will LOVE this. It's almost like a typical pumpkin pie, but when made by Ratha, it's out. Of. This. World! Hopefully you will have similar success!

Crust:
Use your own, a store bought one, or use this graham cracker crust:
¾ cup graham cracker crumbs
¼ granulated brown sugar
½ cup butter, melted

Mix ingredients; press together, then press into the bottom of pie plate. Cook at 350º F for 15 minutes. Remove and cool.

Pumpkin Pie Filling:
1 ½ cups sugar (sometimes she supplements with brown sugar)
2 teaspoons cinnamon
1 teaspoon salt
1 teaspoon ginger
1 teaspoon cloves
4 eggs
4 cups cooked and mashed pumpkin (Ratha always uses fresh)
2 small cans sweetened condensed milk

Whisk eggs in bowl; add other ingredients until well blended. Pour into crust; bake at 350º F for 45–50 minutes.

Ratha's note: Pumpkin pie is best served with friends, family, and whipped cream.

CHAPTER 10:
POST-RESTAURANT

After all four of their children graduated from college, the couple decided they would retire. They sold their restaurant, the Bristol Cafe, to a woman who ran a different, upscale restaurant. During that time, Ratha would go in and help the woman cook Lebanese food. After about one year, business was slow, and the building was sold to another individual, who opened a Chinese restaurant that is still there today—Shanghai, on State Street. The last time we visited in 2023, not too many changes had been made to the interior or exterior of the building, so it was similar to when the Shabeldeens ran it.

For the first several months after the restaurant was closed, Fred and Ratha spent a lot of time together. Ratha would cook. Ratha would clean. Ratha would talk to her Eastern Star friends and prepare for their next meeting or function, perhaps garden outside or prune the plants. While she was doing this, Fred would try to keep himself busy gardening outside. But eventually, he would get bored and follow her around the house, asking her what she was doing. "What are you doing? Why are you doing that? Why are you doing it that way?"

Finally, Ratha got so tired of it she turned to him and stated, "This house isn't big enough for the both of us. One of us has to go out and get a job!" And so it happened.

First, Fred went to work at a local grocery store on Euclid Avenue in Bristol, Virginia. Not only was he hired, but he stayed employed there for twenty years, until he retired for the second time. There, he bagged groceries and stocked shelves. This gave Ratha a short break from him every day. She would wake up, prepare coffee and his breakfast, maybe even pack a lunch for him. He would leave for work and she would clean up, do some laundry, and start preparing for dinner when he would be back home meddling in her business. It's safe to say Ratha stayed home for as long as she could stand it.

So she went down to the lunch counter of a large local department store, HP King and Co.. "Are you hiring?" she asked the kitchen manager. The manager knew Ratha and instructed her not to go anywhere. She went to get her manager and with just one conversation, Ratha was hired to cook at the lunch counter. They asked her if she could start the next day, but Ratha said, "No, I don't want to start that soon." So she compromised and decided to wait for Monday of the following week, three days later, since it was a Friday when she went in. Ratha spent nearly four years working there, learning to cook and prepare lunch foods such as chicken salad, pasta salad, and potato salad. She eventually had to quit when she underwent surgery.

After recovering from the surgery, Ratha started feeling better and was looking for something to do. A friend from Eastern Star reached out and informed her the Virginia School District was looking for a substitute cafeteria worker. Ratha was interested and went to check things out. In no time at all, she was hired as a permanent employee working for the Virginia School System at Virginia High School and substituting in other district schools as well. There, she made rolls, cookies, and breads.

"After I made the rolls, they said 'We can't let you go. You have to stay here.' So I stayed there for ten years, making their breads and rolls—dinner rolls and ham rolls. I made up to eight hundred rolls in one day and sold nearly every single one of them. Those kids," she chuckles "when I made those ham rolls, they bought like five or six of them."

She did this for about ten or eleven years, until she got tired and wanted to retire. So she did, for the second time. Upon her leaving, she tried to teach her replacement how to make the rolls. But Ratha recalls the replacement wasn't interested in watching or learning; she just said, "Rolls, I can make those." The following spring, approximately six months later, Ratha received a phone call from her old manager at the school district asking for help. The manager explained they needed help making rolls, "Just making rolls." So of course, Ratha went in to help. She recalls making the rolls and putting two pans in the oven. When it was time for them to come out of the oven, her hands were full of dough, so she asked another worker to open the oven and remove them before they burned. When the worker opened the oven and saw the rolls, her eyes lit up and she said, "Is that what those rolls are supposed to look like?" And then she laughed. Ratha ended up going back to work for them, just making rolls, for another two years.

"Everywhere I went, I worked hard and did my best. Nobody had ever complained about anything I've done, and I had to learn it on my own."

Meanwhile, just down the road was this young special education teacher working at a nearby middle school. We will call this teacher Miss Carla. Miss Carla, too, loved to cook and bake and had a dream of opening up her own bakery. At first, her vision was of a small bakery where she knew all the locals. Customers would be drawn in by the custom specialized desserts and baked goods that her consumers would claim to die for. She wanted it to have an inviting "coffee shop" environment. Carla dreamed of opening this bakery using many of her mother's recipes.

Although Carla's dreams were of a simpler bakery, her husband wanted to take her dream to the next level. Randall envisioned a bakery that would be open twenty-four hours a day, six days a week. This way, a sweet, delectable treat would be readily available any time of day or night for those that get off work late or arrive to work early. He envisioned an environment with elegant decor, almost as decadent as the desserts themselves, that subliminally invites the customers back again and again for a relaxing and delicious treat. A bakery like that can be not only a part of its community, but earn its place on the map.

But opening a bakery would be a lot of work, especially one

that would be open twenty-four hours a day. Not to mention, Carla wanted to make sure they offered a variety of delicious and decadent dessert specialties. She would need more than just herself, her husband, and her mother's recipes. With Randall being a savvy businessman, the couple started networking and searching for some nearby well-known bakers.

Through a mutual friend, they heard about this woman named Ratha who had built quite a reputation in the community. They met and soon decided that it would be a good fit for both of them to have Ratha join their staff. In 2009, Blackbird Bakery opened in Bristol, Virginia. Ratha started working there when it first opened and continues to do so today.

Initially, Ratha joined the staff of bakers at the new bakery making lemon bars, brownies, and cookies. These were a hit. But Carla also had a demand for pies, so she asked Ratha if she could make some pies as well. At that time, Ratha really hadn't tried to make pies. But like everything else in her life, she could learn. She practiced making her own crust from scratch and experimented with different kinds of pies—fruit, chocolate, coconut, pecan, and more.

While working at the bakery one day, a coworker approached Ratha and asked her, "Ratha, did you see that your pie crust made number one in the state of Virginia?" Ratha had no idea what she was talking about, so the woman pulled out her phone and showed her the online article. There it was: "Number One Pie Crust in the State of Virginia." "No one ever showed me how to make it," Ratha adds. The next day, when she saw Carla's husband, she asked, "Why didn't you tell me my pie crust earned first place? Are you afraid I'll ask you for a raise?" Ratha laughs. "They're the best people to work for." Ratha worked there on and off for the next fifteen years, expanding her baking to include items such as baklava, wedding cookies, and of course those delicious pies with that first-place crust.

Miss Carla's vision of a small local bakery where she knew the names of all her customers was an instant hit. It remained small and personal for a short while, but with Randall's assistance and business expertise, it soon "took off" like a rocket. "Randall is the brains behind its real success. The idea to go twenty-four hours a day was his as well" (Carla Perkins).

Frequently, Miss Carla still swings by Miss Ratha's house in the late morning to pick her up for work. They travel to the bakery together, and Ratha spends four to five hours there baking baklava and wedding cookies. Because Ratha had been gone for a while, and no one else knew how to make baklava as delicious as Ratha's, customers had missed it and were especially excited to see its return. Carla posted about Ratha's visits on social media one day. In that post on Blackbird Bakery's page, there was a photo of Ratha and Fred, as well as photos of the baklava that she just made while there that day. By the end of that week, the post had over 650 likes and a multitude of comments by folks who knew, or knew of, Ratha along the way.

Working at Blackbird Bakery is definitely one of Ratha's favorite post-retirement accomplishments and passions. She is so thrilled that she is able to provide a treat that they love to others. This bakery attracts folks from hundreds of miles away and is talked about all over the East Coast. Once you've stopped by the bakery and experienced its "bakery magic," you will assuredly make it a point to visit it again. The last time I went, I met a couple from Maryland, over four hundred miles away. They said they were driving through on their way back from Florida and make a point of stopping by every time they're close.

VERY CARING CARROT CAKE

One of Ratha's very favorite and most famous cakes is her moist and delicious carrot cake. Try it for yourself!

2 cups all-purpose flour
2 teaspoons baking soda
½ teaspoon salt
2 teaspoons ground cinnamon
1 teaspoon nutmeg
3 eggs, well beaten
¾ cup vegetable oil (or avocado oil, it's extra moist)
¾ cup buttermilk
2 cups sugar
2 teaspoons vanilla extract
1 (8 oz) can crushed pineapple, drained
1 cup grated carrots
½ cup flaked coconut
1 cup chopped walnuts or pecans

1. Combine flour, soda, salt, and cinnamon, mix well. Set aside.

2. In separate bowl, combine eggs, oil, buttermilk, sugar, and vanilla. Beat until smooth.

3. Stir in flour mixture, pineapple, coconut, carrots and chopped nuts, mix well.

4. Pour into two 9-inch greased round pans.

5. Bake at 350° F for 35–40 minutes (until a toothpick comes out clean).

6. Immediately spread buttermilk glaze evenly over layers. Cool for 15 minutes, then remove from pans.

7. Frost with orange cream cheese frosting: in middle, top and sides.

Store cake in refrigerator.

BUTTERMILK GLAZE:

1 cup sugar
½ teaspoon baking soda
½ cup buttermilk
½ cup butter
1 teaspoon vanilla extract
1 tablespoon light corn syrup

Combine all ingredients (except vanilla) in a Dutch oven (or a small pot with lid). Bring to a boil. Cook for 4 additional minutes, stirring constantly. Remove from heat and stir in vanilla.

ORANGE CREAM CHEESE FROSTING

½ cup butter, softened
8 oz cream cheese
1 teaspoon vanilla extract
2 cups sifted powdered sugar
1 teaspoon orange juice
1 tablespoon ground orange rind/zest

Combine butter and cream cheese; mix until light and fluffy. Add vanilla, powdered sugar, juice, and zest. Beat until smooth.

CHAPTER 11:
ONE BIG FAMILY

According to Ratha, family is everything.

But to Ratha, family is also more than just blood relations; they can also include close friends.

"Faithful friends are a sturdy shelter, whoever finds one has found a treasure. Faithful friends are beyond price; no amount can balance their worth. Faithful friends are a life-saving medicine; and those that fear the Lord will find them" (Ecclesiasticus 6:14–16).

Have you ever heard the quote, "It takes a village to raise a child"? Well, this is certainly the case, especially for families immigrating from other countries. What brings people together? Commonality. Similar interests, similar hobbies, similar social groups, as well as common cultural traditions and foods. But more important is need.

So that's what the Shabeldeens had to do—needed to do—make friends. Not just any friends, but faithful, true, lifelong friends. There were many friends from their village and neighboring villages in Lebanon that they met once they got here. Many of these people grew to be close friends and extended family. Most Sundays, the "extended family" tried to get together. The men talked and shared business ideas together. The women told stories, cooked for each other, shared recipes, and gave advice to each other. Most holidays were spent with this extended family. Many of the children grew up to call one another "cousin" or "aunty," even though there was no blood relation there. Miss Ratha is still called "aunty" or "sittie" by many of her best friends' offspring. The Shabeldeens made so many friends in this country over their seventy-eight years here and made an impact on them all.

When her oldest son was in his late teens, he asked his mother, "Are you going to make me marry one of these Lebanese girls?"

Ratha informed him, "No, son. You are going to marry whoever you want to spend your life with. But you are going to choose, not me. I will love whoever you love and loves you."

When they first came to this country, they were young and their firstborn was under two years old. Amidst trying to learn the language, the culture, the transportation system and about the American dollar, they also had to make a living. Throughout their years here in America, they had an additional three children, for a total of four children in the household to raise. Life wasn't easy. It wasn't easy to be a hard worker and an involved parent who supports your children, takes them to sports practices, volunteers at the local high school's snack bar, and more. Such is difficult for most, but even harder for families without grandparents or a lot of family members around, which is why it was important for them to surround themselves with close friends.

When Ratha was a young girl, around five or six years of age, she met another girl from her village with the same first name. They became friends, despite the lack of time they were able to spend together outside of school. They knew each other from the village and tried to make it a point to visit with one another as often as possible. Since she was also called Ratha, we will call her "Ratha A."

When Ratha and Fred moved to America, Fred first started working at a restaurant in Kingsport sixteen hours a day, six days a week. The man that hired him was named Coleman Kassem. Coleman was a fair man to work for. He helped Fred learn the language and introduced him to some of the American traditions and customs. Not only was he a fair and respectable man to work for, he was also single and wanted a family. Ratha used to tease him that he should go to Lebanon and meet her (only) childhood friend, Ratha Abulhusn (Ratha A.). After months and months of back-and-forth chatting, Mr. Kassem did plan a trip to Lebanon. He planned a trip to meet, and eventually marry, Ratha A.

When Ratha A. migrated to America to join her American

husband, she kept in close contact with her childhood friend, Miss Ratha. The two ladies would get together on weekends for family picnics at the park during the summertime and at one of their houses during inclement weather. While the two were not blood related, their children referred to one another as "cousins." Coleman was also able to be a support for Fred during his journey as a husband, a father, and a future restaurant owner. The friendships between these two families were deep—definitely a shelter and a lasting treasure.

Although loving her neighbors and making friends was easy for Ratha, raising her own children was a tad more challenging. Her children watched how hard she worked for her family. They witnessed some of the unfaithfulness, as well as the verbal and physical abuse experienced in the beginning. Working hard to support your family and keeping your family intact requires great perseverance, more perseverance than most of us have today.

Ratha may have been gone to work in the mornings when the children woke for school, but she was still very present. They knew to get ready under Fred's guidance and that their mother would prepare a hot breakfast for them they would enjoy on the bus. Each day, Ratha gave the bus driver a sack of hot breakfasts to feed them when they got on to go to school in the mornings. Even though she arrived at the restaurant by 5:30 a.m. every day, she arranged with the bus driver to stop by the restaurant in the mornings where she would run out a load of hot breakfasts to him—one for each of her school-aged children and one for the driver.

The aforementioned saying, "it takes a village to raise a child," has even more meaning when you have multiple children, are here from another country, and don't have parents or siblings around to help support you or be responsible, adult confidants to your children. And this is absolutely true with this hard-working family. To this day, Ratha can recall many people in their small community who positively influenced her children, who talked with them, guided them, listened to them, took them to practice, and even counseled them when needed. But this couple took care of business at home as well as at the restaurant; they didn't let just anyone influence their children. This is why Ratha always enjoyed the children being at home, with their friends visiting. That way, she knew where they were and could keep an eye on them. Not to mention, the friends usually got to enjoy some amazing meal that made them sure to come back for more.

Not that long ago, when Ratha was at a local establishment, an aged woman came up to her and asked, "Ms. Shabeldeen?" Ratha didn't recognize her, but it turned out this woman was one of her daughter's friends from high school who used to visit with the family and join them for dinner. Ratha knew that making meals was a way to show love, a way to build memories and warm both the heart and the stomach. She knew these children, along with her own, would grow up with amazing memories of gathering around the table to talk, fellowship, laugh and enjoy mouthwatering meals.

With both of their businesses, the Bristol Cafe and the Coffee Cup (owned and operated separately, at two different locations and times), the Shabeldeens were in business for approximately fifty years. A large majority of their customers were local police officers whose offices were across the street. Many of these officers were not only customers but also helped with the children as well as helped Ratha get to work when she didn't have a car.

"They helped me raise my family," Ratha brags.

Some of the officers became close confidantes of the family. The children would specifically and frequently ask where Officer Mumprew was or when he would be in. Officer Mumprew would chat with the children, listen to their stories, wipe tears from their faces, and give solid advice.

Ratha and Fred came to this country with their oldest son, Sammy. Throughout the years, they had two more boys and one daughter, for a total of four children. To this day, Ratha will say that raising boys is significantly easier than raising girls. "Boys can play, but the girls? They have to pay." You have to protect your girls much more than you do the boys. You have to be vigilant about who they hang out with and what kinds of crowds and boys they are going out with. She also adds that her teenage boys always wanted to stay home; they were the happiest when Mom would come home and cook dinner for them. If you have ever had a teenage daughter, perhaps you noticed they're more adventurous and want to try more things—new things such as going out to eat, going to new places, and exploring with friends. They want to get out of the house just to get out of the house.

As mentioned, Ratha had only one daughter. She always wanted to work and visited shop owners asking for jobs since before she was old enough to work. When she was about fifteen, she had formed a good friendship with some girls who lived down the street from the Shabeldeens at that time. The girls were from a household full of other children. One of those children was a twenty-one-year-old boy who had his eye on Ratha's daughter, Deanne.

Deanne liked the attention and enjoyed spending time at the other family's house. There she could be "free" with all the other kids hanging around, without chores or responsibilities, and no parent breathing down her neck. Ratha wasn't happy about this, as she knew the reputation of the family, as well as the fact that Deanne pretty much disappeared and spent most of her time there. When she was looking for her, Ratha would call the household and inquire about her daughter's whereabouts. The "mother" or female adult in the house would lie to Ratha, telling her they didn't know where Deanne was. Ratha knew these were lies. Once, she drove to the house with a police officer and retrieved her daughter after such a phone call.

As with many strong-willed teenage girls, the more you warn them about something, the more appeal and interest they find in what you're warning them of. Deanne was very interested in hanging out with this family and the twenty-one-year-old boy who was trying to date her. Ratha knew the boy's mother was speaking poorly about Ratha behind her back to Deanne and felt the woman wanted Deanne to move there with them and participate in some of the illegal activities she had heard about.

It was during this time period when the restaurant was frequented by all the small town's policemen; they all knew Fred and Ratha fairly well and had tremendous respect for the couple. When Ratha told them who Deanne was dating, they shook their heads and told her the boy's family was not good news. Ratha shared this "opinion" with her daughter, who felt the initial desire to rebel. She threatened to leave the house and accused her mother of being too "controlling." Ratha agreed, saying, "You can leave the house. But first, we have to stop at the police station and we can sign some paperwork."

At the police station, Ratha sat with a lieutenant at the front office. She explained to him everything that was going on. He asked that he pull her into his office and have a serious conversation with her and explain exactly what she was getting herself into. Ratha did not agree. "I do not want to be a part of that conversation. She needs to see it outside of my eyes and away from me. She needs to hear it for herself, from someone else." So the lieutenant asked Ratha to send her daughter in so he could have a chat with her. Ratha did, and stayed outside. While in the office, we don't know exactly what was said to Deanne or what evidence she was able to be exposed to. But when she walked out of the office over an hour later, she ran down the hallway towards her mother, with tears in her eyes. "I'm so sorry, Momma! I'm so sorry! I didn't know what that family was really like!" After that, their daughter was much closer to her mother. She looked at her mother with newfound respect, and from then on, paid better attention to her guidance.

Many years later as a young adult, Deanne was dating a boy from the area who was from a wealthy family. Ratha assumed he had his share of ex-girlfriends and that he wanted her daughter to be his next conquest. Ratha also assumed he was used to getting whatever he wanted, including the girls. She saw him as the type of boy who would date a girl for a bit and then dump her when he was through. Deanne had dated this boy for a while and really liked him. When he brought up the topic of moving in together, Deanne considered the proposition, until her mother found out about it.

"When I found out she wanted to move in with him, I had to sit down and have a conversation with him. I told him he can't use my daughter like that. His response was that I couldn't tell my daughter what to do."

Ratha's response: "If she is going to call herself my daughter, then yes, I can."

Deanne was a motivated, strong-willed, and hard-working young woman. She was close to her mother and respected her. So did her boyfriend. Within six months, they were married and, like all the other Shabeldeen children, they still are.

Family is everything to Ratha. They are her pride and joy. She brags about her children's hard work and their accomplishments. She is proud that none of her family members have ever been divorced and they all have a college education.

Life wasn't easy for either of them, but especially for Ratha. She stuck to her fundamental values, that her children would be raised with both a mother and a father, no matter what. She did have to work hard and put up with a lot, but through it all, she taught Fred how to be an amazing man and a good husband.

Recently, her son Sam commented to her, "We never could have done it without you."

For many years, there was a family tradition where all the family came together at the Shabeldeen home at least two times a year: Christmas and the Fourth of July. As many as twenty-three people would come to spend a few nights in their 1700 square foot house. Every single bedroom was full, and all the grandchildren slept together in two rooms, with others on couches and on the floor, staying up all night talking, laughing, telling stories, and making memories. These yearly reunions helped the family stay close and connected. Ratha enjoyed cooking for them and preparing meals of sandwiches, pies, tabouli, and a variety of other Lebanese and American dishes. One of their favorite activities was going to the park, where they would picnic, watch fireworks, go for hikes and walks, search for crawdads, play volleyball and other outdoor games. These were probably the most cherished days of Ratha's life, when she could see what all their hard work had resulted in: a close family.

EASY PEASY SWEET CHESS PIE

"This is the best pie ever!" (Ratha Shabeldeen)

Generations ago, sweet chess pie was popular in the south because cooks found it both easy and economical, with most all the ingredients right there on the farm. Ratha claims this to be the best pie ever, but it's really up to every person's individual taste. This is a sweet but smooth, almost milky textured pie. Try it and let us know what you think!

2 cups sugar
2 tablespoons all-purpose flour
5 large eggs, lightly beaten
⅔ cup buttermilk
½ cup butter, melted
1 teaspoon vanilla extract
1 unbaked 9-inch pastry pie shell

Add sugar and flour in a large mixing bowl; add eggs and buttermilk, stir until blended well.

Stir in butter and vanilla; pour into unbaked pastry shell/crust.

Bake at 350° F for 45 minutes or until pie is set.

CHAPTER 12:
THE BIONIC WOMAN

"I've had three shoulder surgeries, a knee replacement, a hip replacement, and an eye replacement," Ratha brags.

"When you meet trials of various kinds, for you know that the testing of your faith produces steadfastness. And let steadfastness have its full effect, that you may be perfect and complete, lacking in nothing" (James 1:2–4).

Obviously, she isn't bragging, but in a weird way, she is. When she tells of her ailments and physical tribulations in life, she is so proud and feels so blessed to have overcome them all. Hearing of all her many physical ailments and hardships would probably make you think she is crippled, blind, disabled, or perhaps even deceased. But not this woman. She worked through each ailment/issue with perseverance, faith, and without stopping work. If you could see this (now) ninety-some-year-old woman, you would smile. She is an active, BEAMING, feisty and vivacious woman who doesn't want to be waited on and barely accepts help with anything. She cooks and cleans; she goes shopping and carries her groceries into the house. Not to mention, she goes up and down the stairs multiple times a day, as she lives in the downstairs/basement portion of her house.

Don't get me wrong. She definitely has her bad days where she stays in bed, or rubs arthritis medicine on her shoulder or feet, or forgets to take a medicine and gets dizzy (and has fallen a few times). However, she doesn't let those ailments slow her down or stop her. She will rest, but then get up and keep on going.

How can a ninety-year-old woman do so much? Good question! Perhaps her perseverance, perhaps her stubbornness, perhaps her work ethic and inner strength. If you ask her, she will say, "God is good. God has always been good to me." God is good and has helped her get through every aspect of her life, including some amazing recoveries and healings.

Like many other people in their early fifties, Ratha developed a cataract in one of her eyes. A family friend recommended a doctor who was located at a special hospital in a neighboring city for eye surgery. When the doctor saw her eye, he agreed she had a cataract, and said she needed surgery to remove it. She had surgery on her left eye. She went home soon after to recover and had immediate adverse reactions, including a severe headache and intense light sensitivity.

A week later, she had to go back to the doctor for a check-up, but the headache was persistent and the sensitivity to light exceptionally painful. Her daughter had to put a bag over her head to block the light out and drive her there. The pain was so intense she could barely tolerate it. They had to drive forty-five minutes to get to the doctor's office, and when they rolled up into the parking lot (one week after her surgery), the office informed her that the doctor had retired. So she was forced to see some of the other physicians who had no idea what could be wrong or causing her so much pain and discomfort. Despite many office visits, they could never diagnose or rectify the problem.

She continued having chronic and severe headaches for several months before she was finally able to get into a specialist in Knoxville. Because she didn't want to drive that far with only one eye, not to mention all the pain she was in, she had to rely on her neighbors and friends to transport her. At the specialist, they gave her some type of prescription eye drops, which seemed to lighten the pain a bit. She continued these trips to the specialist in Knoxville for almost twenty years. She grew tired of the cyclical and nonresponsive treatment and started being more demanding with her questions. What was wrong? How were they preparing to resolve it properly? But instead of answering her questions, she was continually transferred from one doctor to another. All with no answers, diagnosis, or explanations. She recalls walking into a new doctor's office once to have the eye examined. After he took a look at her eye, he shook his head. She knew someone had really messed up—undoubtedly the first doctor that performed the surgery. She knew that it was only out of professional courtesy that he didn't bad-mouth the prior doctor. But he, like the rest, tried to find a way to stop her pain and save her vision.

Ratha continued seeing specialist after specialist. She was misguided into thinking her eye was getting better, which is what kept her coming back to the doctors for so many years. Instead of healing, however, her eye was continuing to get worse. Ratha did not know at the time the doctor that performed her cataract surgery had damaged her optical nerve, called optical nerve atrophy. "Atrophy" means wasting away and yes, it was her optical nerve that was deteriorating. This condition happens as a result of long-term damage to the optic nerve fibers. The damage this causes to your vision is not only irreversible but progressive and often leads to blindness.

While in the waiting room one day, sitting and patiently waiting for her appointment, Ratha noticed a woman in the waiting room staring at her intently. So intently that Ratha couldn't help but notice. Finally, the woman broke the awkward silence and asked, "Were you born with one brown and one blue eye?" Ratha wanted to laugh. Then she wanted to cry. She wanted to scream out in desperation, anguish, and frustration. But she didn't. She calmly stated, "No, honey, I was born with two brown eyes. But I'm having trouble with the blue one, which is why I am here."

Finally, after some twenty years of making long road trips to the doctor's office at least twice a month, Ratha started demanding answers. They informed her that they would need to perform surgery. She didn't like this, as surgery is what started all of this in the first place. So she asked to be transferred to a closer physician, some 30 miles away instead of the 120 miles she had been traveling all this time. They gave her the referral she had asked for to a doctor who didn't have any more medical knowledge or answers to this dire situation than the previous doctors. However, he did offer more honesty and bluntness.

She started seeing the local doctor for several months, but

the crippling pain and light sensitivity continued with no relief. The only thing that provided a small amount of relief were eye drops, but they were just a temporary relief. They never completely numbed the pain, and as soon as the drops wore off, the pain became unbearable. It took him a while, but the doctor finally became brutally honest and blunt with her. He informed her that she had optical nerve damage and that this nerve damage had been and was continuing to get progressively worse. "Ms. Shabeldeen, your eye isn't going to get better. We have tried everything we know of. We need to take your eye out." Imagine that. Just imagine a doctor telling you that you would need to lose an eye! You would probably do exactly what she did; she started crying and walked right out of the doctor's office. She left without saying a word.

She stayed away from doctors for as long as she could until she had another episode of severe headaches so bad she couldn't ignore them anymore. She wasn't even able to leave the house without an eye patch and a paper bag over her head. It was so bad all she could think of doing was to go to the emergency room, so she did one afternoon. There, the emergency room doctor informed her they couldn't do anything for her and that she would need to return to her eye specialist. It was at that point that Ratha realized she couldn't evade the eye specialist anymore. She didn't like what he was saying to her, but she also couldn't live with this pain. This was making her life intolerable.

So she went back to the specialist and made an appointment to have her eye taken out. The process involved different steps, but all were done in a clinic, and she was home in the afternoon. The first step was that she had to have her eye removed from the socket. As she went home to recover, the doctor had to measure her eye and wait for a replacement eye to be manufactured. During this time, she had to wear sunglasses and an eye patch.

Putting the replacement eye in was another one day, in-and-out procedure. On the first try, the replacement eye was a success! It fit perfectly and it matched her other eye beautifully. The surgery was quick, followed by a short visit in the recovery room. When she finally walked out of the surgery room, the office staff stood up, gathered around her, and gave her a standing ovation, followed by a big celebration. Everyone cheered and clapped. They hugged her and cried tears of happiness with her. She can still recall the immense sense of happiness and pride she felt to have two eyes again. Her fake eye looks almost identical to the other, with the same coloring. As a matter of fact, if you didn't know she had a fake eye, you wouldn't be able to tell. What a blessing.

Years later, a twelve-year-old neighbor boy across the street came to visit with Ratha. He showed her a new trick he had learned at school. Ratha told him she had a new trick as well. The boy inquired, "What's your trick?"

Ratha replied, "I can take my eye out," and started gesturing as if she was about to.

The boy screamed, "No! No! I don't want to see that!" as they both started laughing together.

Many years earlier, in her late twenties, she was washing the windows in her upstairs apartment. She stood on the banister/handrail, and then she fell. As she fell, she naturally turned her body a bit and landed on her side. Once down, she was frozen with pain. The doctor told her she pulled the ligament in her hip but that it would heal. He gave her crutches and told her to stay off her leg. But with three kids and a business to run, she couldn't. So she used the crutches to go up and down the stairs every day to get to work. At that time, they were living in an apartment above the restaurant. Approximately three to four times a day, she would have to leave work, go up the stairs to the second-floor apartment to check on the kids or feed them. She did have a woman who helped come over and watch the children, but that wasn't full time. So she would go up to cook for them and then rest a bit before making the long haul back down the stairs to return to the restaurant. After several weeks passed, the pain was still excruciating, and her movement was limited. So she went back to the doctor and this time, he informed her that she had a torn ligament in her hip, which would need surgery to heal.

What choice did she have? Not really any. So she had the surgery, but first she had to hire a waitress at the restaurant to help while she was out. Three days after surgery, she was back at work on her crutches. (She had gotten pretty mobile on them by then, apparently.) She hobbled around on those crutches for about six weeks, but eventually recovered fully.

"I walked home many days and wore my knee out," says Miss Ratha.

Ratha blames her bum knee on all the walking she did. As a child, she worked in the fields and in America she walked to and from work every day, saving all her pennies, dimes, and nickels so they could buy a house. So it was no surprise to her when her knee went out and the doctors said she needed knee surgery.

In addition to all that, she had a big toe that turned and started growing underneath her little toe. It was getting painful and to the point where she couldn't wear shoes. So she went to the doctor, who said she needed surgery to fix it. During surgery, he broke the big toe, moved it so it would no longer go underneath the other toe, and put it back together with screws. After that surgery, her toes were straight again, and she was able to wear shoes once again.

There was about a ten-year period when she had ongoing stomach issues and pain. Her doctor told her to take antacid tablets, but the stomach issues never got better. Finally, after years and years of complaining at doctor visits, she got really sick and couldn't tolerate the pain anymore, so she had a friend take her to urgent care. At the urgent care, they told her she needed to go to the hospital. The doctors in the emergency room then told her that her gall bladder had exploded and released toxins into her body. And if this wasn't bad enough, a gallstone was somewhere in her body. They vigorously treated her with antibiotics and had to play the waiting game. Four days later, her toxin levels were low enough that they could do surgery on her, and they removed the gallstone. When they pulled it out, the surgeons said it had been in her body for so long that it had completely rotted.

"For ten years, I complained to my doctor about my stomach. When he came in to visit me after the surgery, I reminded him that I've been dealing with that stomach pain for ten years. The doctor turned around and walked out of the room without saying a word." (For inquiring minds, Ratha never did see that doctor again.)

Ratha had issues with her shoulder as well. She went to the doctor and told them she had been experiencing severe shoulder pain for quite some time. The doctor informed her that she needed to have surgery on her shoulder. That first surgery didn't go as planned and left her in worse pain than before. After her second shoulder surgery, she still had an immense amount of pain. The doctor told her she would need to stay home and go on disability because she would never be able to use her shoulder again. (Keep in mind that there are many folks who beg their doctors to put them on disability; they look forward to the leniency of not having to work.) But not Ratha. After hearing this comment from her doctor, she told him, "You fix my shoulder. I'll show you if I can use it or not." So she had her third surgery and a few weeks later went back to work at the restaurant, cooking, lifting, cleaning, and serving. It was a bit painful she admits, but she didn't let it slow her down. Then again, not much slowed her down. At her follow-up visit, the doctor was in awe. He commented, "I've never seen anyone like that before." And he probably never did again.

ITALIAN CREAM CAKE

I found this very old handwritten recipe in Miss Ratha's recipe book. It caught my eye because of the name—I am Italian and proud. I learned that "oleo" refers to a fatty substance or oil and can include margarine.

5 eggs, separated
2 cups sugar
1 stick oleo (margarine or ½ cup vegetable oil)
½ cup Crisco
2 teaspoon vanilla
1 teaspoon baking soda
1 cup buttermilk
2 cups flour
1 can coconut (or substitute with 1 cup dry flakes)
First, beat egg whites until fluffy.

Then, cream together:
1 stick oleo
½ cup Crisco
5 egg yolks
1 teaspoon vanilla

1. In separate bowl, mix buttermilk, baking soda, and 1 teaspoon vanilla until thoroughly blended.

2. Add 2 cups flour.

3. Fold in beaten egg whites.

4. Fold in coconut.

5. Pour into greased cake pan(s); bake at 350° F about 35–40 minutes or until done. (Insert toothpick; if it comes out clean, cake is done.)

CHAPTER 13:
EARNED IT!

"God guided me every step of the way. I thank Him every night and every single day" (Ratha Shabeldeen).

Her son told her, "With what you learned since you've been in this country— You've taught yourself how to read, how to cook, how to quilt, and you've earned everything by yourself. There is no such thing as can't."

"Everything in life I had to learn, on my own. But I was determined to do it. I wanted to show what I could do by myself" (Ratha Shabeldeen).

By now, you have a fairly good understanding of who Ratha is and what her life consisted of, including her work ethic, her family, her trials and tribulations, and her faith. Her whole life story is one of hard work; nothing was ever given to her (except a husband that she didn't even want at the age of thirteen). But she took her adverse situations and made the most out of them— made lemonade out of lemons, as some say. She taught herself how to read, how to cook, how to hold her head up high, how to be assertive, and how to be respected by others. But everything in life, she earned.

As a young girl, she had to work in the fields behind the plow in her father's fields and help take care of her younger cousins. She was laughed at and mocked, constantly. All day and every day, fingers pointed at her saying how fat she was, how ugly she was, how awkward she was, how she did things the wrong way (after people showed her to do things the wrong way), and how stupid she was. Coming to America, she had nothing but a small child to care for and a husband who could barely provide. She learned the language; she learned a trade; she networked with people to build a successful business and maintained the respect of her customers, members of her community, and everyone she met. When Fred would talk poorly of some customers, she would gently remind him, "They put the food on the table and in the mouths of your children. You show respect to them."

When customers would flirt with her, she would react sternly but with dignity, "Keep your hands off. I don't belong to you." She had the respect of her customers because she earned it. She walked miles and miles to work so she could save her bus money and make a down payment on a house. Everything they had, they worked for and earned. She opened the restaurant six days a week, starting at 5:30 in the morning, to prepare meals for that day and the next. Everything she had, she earned.

One very common question people ask about God is: Does He have a sense of humor? I say, especially after hearing this next story, He absolutely does.

It was late one summer afternoon and Fred and Ratha were going to bring their grandson a used car for his birthday. Fred was to drive the new car, and Ratha was to drive the family car behind him. Fred warned her to be very careful about the road conditions and warned her not to get lost. "Make sure you stay behind me because you will get lost once we get into Charlotte. There are a lot of crazy streets there." Ratha understood and made sure she followed his directions and stayed behind him.

Once they were in Charlotte, they got lost, even though Fred was leading the way. They drove around the small-town roads and finally found their way back to the interstate. The speed limit on the small-town roads was 45 or less; but when they entered the interstate, the speed changed to 65. Ratha continued to follow Fred, who was still driving 45 mph. After following him for several miles, she finally decided she would pass him to let him know the speed limit had increased. As she passed him on the left, he began beeping his horn at her. He continued to beep and was waving her down, insinuating he wanted her to pull over. Once they pulled over, Fred got out of the car and yelled at her for not following him. He warned her she was going too fast and was going to end up getting a ticket.

"I won't get a ticket. I'm just driving the speed limit," she exclaimed. He wouldn't hear it, and just insisted she was to follow him so she didn't get a speeding ticket. "We can't get a speeding ticket! You'll get your license taken away!" he continued. So they got back in their vehicles, Fred pulled out first and Ratha followed, now traveling 65 mph.

When they got close to their destination, they parked the newer vehicle at a Walmart. They wrapped a big ribbon around it and left it in the parking lot, going together in their own car to their son and grandson's house nearby. Once they got there, Fred wasn't feeling well and needed medication that he said was only sold at Walmart. None of the family knew what was going on, except for Fred and Ratha. So everyone piled in the car, and they drove to Walmart. Once there, they noticed the spectacle of the car oddly wrapped in a ribbon. They parked close by to "check it out." Fred gave his grandson the key and told him to see if it opened the door. His grandson stared at him, and he said, "Papa! You can't do that!"

Fred responded with, "Well, if it doesn't open it, then it's not meant to be. There's no harm in trying."

So he handed young Dean the keys, and when he went to the door and found out the key actually opened it, his jaw dropped in disbelief and everyone else (in on the secret now) sang Happy Birthday to him.

When it was time to go home, Fred told Ratha he would drive because "You're a hot rod driver and you're going to get us a speeding ticket." She nodded her head in compliance and gave the keys to Fred.

On the way home, guess who got a speeding ticket? Yes, indeed, Fred. After chastising and ridiculing her for not following him and driving too fast (or faster than he was), he was the one who got the speeding ticket. Was it karma? Or was it God? People do say God has a sense of humor.

After that event, Fred never drove again. It wasn't until after this event that Ratha finally earned the recognition as a respected driver in Fred's eyes. It took all of this, and plenty of years, for her to earn it. At least she finally did.

"Everything in life, I had to earn," she continually states. When she says everything, she means everything, including respect from her husband.

One December morning in 2021, Fred didn't get out of bed. He claimed he wasn't feeling well. As a matter of fact, he didn't get out of bed for the next couple of days. Ratha and the family recommended he go see a doctor, but he refused. Ratha noticed how difficult it was for him to get up and use the restroom, and he didn't even try to shower. Was it a cold? The flu or Covid? He didn't have a cough, just random symptoms. On the third day, a family friend came over and called 911. The emergency operator asked what his blood sugar was, since he was a diabetic. They tested it and it was exceptionally high—above 400. The operator told the family not to do anything, not even to give him a shot of insulin until the ambulance got there. They dispatched an ambulance and said they would transport him to the hospital.

Perhaps Fred knew better, as he pleaded with his family and caretakers to give him a shot. But the family vowed to listen to the emergency operator. An ambulance soon arrived and escorted him to the local hospital. At the hospital, Ratha sat by his bedside and held his hand, crying and worried about her husband. It hit her then that this was not just her husband; he was her life partner, her cousin, her best friend, and her life companion. He lay with his eyes closed most of the time. Her mind was flooded with memories—memories of their childhood; memories of their life together; memories of raising the children; memories of planting, gardening, laughing, and building a life together. Fred had been in her life since she could remember, all the way back to the toddler days. As a matter of fact, she couldn't recall a day without him.

Suddenly, while lying in the hospital bed next to where she was sitting and leaning over by his side, his eyes opened. He looked at his wife, who was staring lovingly back at him. Who knows what he was thinking as he looked lovingly at his first cousin, his life companion, his best friend, and his wife? His eyes softened and then sparkled as he gently smiled at her. He started talking, and Ratha had to lean closer in order to hear him.

As she leaned in just close enough to hear the whispering words flow from his mouth, she heard, "I love you, and I'm sorry." He took a deep breath as his eyes closed for the very last time.

She had never heard those words before; it took over seventy-five years of marriage for Fred to finally tell Ratha he loved her. But after more than seventy-five years of living, working, laughing, arguing, surviving good times and bad times and making a life together, she finally heard those words every woman is desperate to hear. She had finally earned his love.

RATHA'S HOMEMADE PIZZA

Dough:
3 ½ cups flour
1 tablespoon yeast

Sift together. Then add:
2 teaspoons salt
2 tablespoons salad oil
2 cups water

(If it's too soft, add more flour.)

Mix ingredients. Place a wet towel over the bowl and place on/near the stovetop to rise for 1 to 2 hours. While the dough is rising, fry hamburger and make sauce.

Pizza Sauce:
1 can of tomato sauce
1 can tomato paste
1 tablespoon oregano
½ teaspoon pepper
1 tablespoon Italian seasoning
Optional/recommended pizza toppings:
1 lb. cooked ground beef (or Italian sausage)
Sliced pepperoni
Mozzarella cheese, shredded (1–2 cups)

After dough rises, roll into a flat shape as desired; about ½ inch thick. Rub olive oil over top of pizza (about 1–2 tablespoons) and sprinkle some mozzarella cheese. Then put sauce over cheese, sprinkle more mozzarella cheese, then add cooked hamburger and pepperoni, if desired.

Bake at 425° F for 25–30 minutes, until dough turns a golden brown. Remove and let cool for 5 minutes.

CHAPTER 14:
POSTSCRIPT

After Fred passed in 2021, Ratha's life abruptly changed. Not only did she have to learn how to live without him, she also had to learn how to be by herself. At no point in her life had she ever been alone. She also had to learn how to do things like register the car, pay the insurance, pay the electricity and phone bills, as well as hire people to perform services. She had to learn to rely on friends to do some of the things Fred used to do. But worst of all, Ratha had to learn to be alone. It wasn't until Fred's passing that she realized she had never been alone. She went from living with her aunt and uncle in a big house full of cousins to having a family of her own and caring for them. Her days at the restaurant were full of chatting with customers and other employees. After Fred was gone, Ratha began to realize how long the nights really were, how scary the creaks in the house in the middle of the night could be, and how terrifying the silence was. For the first time in her life, Ratha felt alone.

Many evenings she broke down and cried, calling her children and friends in tears, panicked and humbled by her anxiety. The family gathered to discuss what to do next. Should she move to be with one of them? Each of her four children live out of state—and in different states. So they each took turns having her come visit for a while, for about a month or so. Soon enough, it became evident there was a clear pattern: she got there and was full of energy and excitement. She spent the first week or two loving on her grandchildren and enjoying her time with family. About two weeks into the visit, she began to lose her enthusiasm. She became lost and out of place, as if she realized she might be a burden on her busy family members. She missed her home; she missed her routines; she missed her space; she missed her quietness; she missed her friends stopping by to visit; she missed seeing people she knew at church or in the grocery store; and she missed her kitchen. Oh, how she missed her kitchen! There is nothing like trying to cook in someone else's kitchen; it's just not the same. Eventually, she would ask to be taken home so she could return to what she knew.

After returning home, she would be excited and enjoy the familiar setting and her kitchen. Yes, especially her kitchen, where she knew where all her cooking utensils were, where all the ingredients were, and she did not have to worry about messing up someone else's kitchen. Yet soon enough, the cycle would repeat. The loneliness would creep in, the fear of the unknown in the middle of the night, and the panic of "what if" took a toll on her. Or at least until the next time she went to stay with one of her children. The family talked about selling the house and moving her in with one of them. Sometimes she agreed, but would soon change her mind. She didn't want to give up the house she raised her family in, the house she knew, and the forever house she and Fred worked hard to purchase.

Ratha was able to handle most household chores by herself or with the help of her neighbor and friend, Carolyn. Carolyn was not only a neighbor but also a retired nurse who was twenty years younger than Ratha. She lived a few houses away and had been helping the Shabeldeens for the past decade by driving them places and helping to take care of Fred with his diabetes. She also helped them keep up with their bills, reminding them about appointments, events, and many other essentials. Most important, she was a good friend, who would both call and visit several times a day. Carolyn bought Ratha a deck of Skip-Bo cards, and now it has become a favorite hobby to play at least a few hands every day. But Carolyn couldn't be there all the time to take care of the chores and tasks that needed to be done or to keep Ratha company 24/7.

One afternoon, Ratha was carrying a bag of trash to the garbage can up the back stairs outside. Her foot tangled around the bag, and she fell. Like most people, she thought, "It's not that bad." She took a moment to catch her breath, rolled over on her side, and used the iron banisters on the side of the steps to help her pull herself up. She limped into the house and lay down for a while. A few hours later, she called her friend Carolyn from down the street and told her what had happened, saying she couldn't walk and her knee was swollen.

Against her wishes, Carolyn took Ratha to the emergency room where they x-rayed and MRI'd her knee and leg. Fortunately, it was nothing serious. But it brought light to the pending doom of what about next time? Ratha couldn't keep carrying things up and down the stairs as she tends to do. (Nor should she prune her rose bushes, but no one can really stop her from doing that either.) What if? What if her fall was so bad she couldn't get herself up? What if she breaks something? She would surely have to be put in some kind of assisted living setting, and she would hate it. Not being able to have access to her kitchen or have her family or friends from years past stop by to visit would be a death sentence for this spunky and active ninety-three-year-old woman who loves people and loves having a social life. What should they do?

The family suggested to Ratha that she move into a senior center or a care facility that would remind her to take her medicine. This would also eliminate the chores around the house that could potentially be dangerous, like carrying a bag of trash out or a basket of laundry upstairs. Ratha didn't want that. Too reclusive and no one would know where to find her, as she is still well known throughout the community.

What about a program like Visiting Angels or an organization that sent out caretakers to visit with and help solo seniors with chores like shopping, cleaning, grocery shopping, and companionship? Ratha didn't want to have to pay someone to visit with her, especially when she already had so many friends and family members stopping in to visit. Of course, the family couldn't argue with their strong-willed mother. But the problem remained: these visits were not consistent and there were many periods of time that she was alone.

Because her father was a Mason, Ratha had been a part of the Eastern Star organization for years. It can be said that "the members of the Order of the Eastern Star are dedicated men and women who sincerely reflect the spirit of fraternal love and the desire to work together for good by giving their time to meaningful projects that benefit mankind" (https://easternstar.org/about-oes). Aside from socializing and baking pies for the other ladies to enjoy, Ratha's favorite part of the meetings was her "job." Her job was to carry the American flag into the room, down the center of the aisle, at the beginning of each meeting. When she talks about this, you can see her strong sense of patriotism and respect for her country, the United States of America.

Ratha joined this organization for many reasons: to meet and network with other local women and to work on charitable events and deeds, as well as to help her feel connected to her dad. That, I believe, was the strongest reason why she joined.

While venting her fears to some friends during a meeting one afternoon, one of her friends, Miss Dot, spoke up. "I'll come live with you. I'll live with you and help take care of you. I can help you clean, shop, and make sure you're eating and taking care of yourself." Miss Dorothy stepped up to the plate. Dorothy had been a long-time friend of Ratha's from Eastern Star, and the ladies had known each other for about twenty years. Dot is a country girl who was born and raised in the backwoods of Virginia. She was married twice, but left the first husband and the second husband died. She was living in a house by herself and spent much time visiting with friends and helping take care of them by doing errands like shopping, laundry, cleaning the house, etc.

Ironically, she was three years Ratha's senior. This made the family wonder a bit. How could a ninety-six-year-old woman help out their ninety-three-year-old mother? Ratha was excited about the opportunity to have her friend come stay with her, but her family was a bit hesitant. Who was this woman? Did she have an ulterior motive? What if she wasn't as capable of caring for

Ratha, or even herself, as she claimed to be? What if she gets hurt and falls herself? What if she ends up having more issues than their mom? What if they argue? What if she moves in and they can't get rid of her? What if, what if...? The family had multiple questions, concerns, and inquiries. But their mother insisted. "Dot is going to come live with me and help take care of me."

Miss Dot had spent many years of her life "caring" for others in their homes, as well as working at a nursing facility as a nurse's assistant. She also had a good sense of humor, which would help Ratha laugh. So she moved in and provided companionship for Ratha. The two ladies seemed to enjoy most of their time together. Eventually, however, they started arguing and getting annoyed with one another. It was difficult for Ratha to have raised her family, her business, and have cared for her husband for so many years and then have someone come into her house and tell her what to do. So that living situation didn't last very long. Women will be women, even in their nineties. They will be strong-willed, sometimes bossy if not mean, get their feelings hurt, and say things perhaps they wish they hadn't. After a few months, both the ladies agreed it would be in their best interests to maintain their own residences and have Dot move out. This would be the best way to continue their friendship. Having a roommate can be difficult, at any age.

A few days after Miss Dot moved out, Ratha stated, "I feel as if I have my freedom back. I wasn't free in my home. I couldn't do what I wanted to do or even what I had been doing for years!" Although still a bit lonely, she currently lives alone, but appreciates her freedom and all she has.

"I don't have a lot, but there is nothing more I need. I have my family, my friends, and my neighbors. I love every single one of them."

Now that you have read about and learned some of Miss Ratha's life, I encourage you to go back to the very beginning of this book and reread "The Virtuous Wife" from Proverbs 31.

Does it seem a tad different to you now than when you first read it? Do you see any resemblances to the biblical ideal of a virtuous wife in Miss Ratha? God works in mysterious ways, and I claim to know nothing of His mysteries or majesty. But one thing I know for sure is this: despite Ratha's tribulations and struggles, God has worked in her and with her throughout her whole life. If you are blessed enough to have known her at some point, I am positive you will agree.

GERMAN CHOCOLATE PECAN BARS

Let's end this story of a sweet woman with one of her sweetest recipes!

3 cups of pecan halves or pieces
1 ¾ cups all-purpose flour
¾ cup powdered sugar
¾ cup butter, cubed
¼ cup unsweetened, sifted cocoa
1 ½ cups semisweet chocolate morsels
¾ cup firmly packed brown sugar
¾ cup light corn syrup
¼ cup butter, melted
3 large eggs, lightly beaten
1 cup sweetened coconut flakes

Preheat oven to 350° F.

Bake pecans on a shallow cookie sheet for 8 minutes (place in a single layer).

Line bottom and sides of a 13 x 9-inch pan with heavy duty aluminum foil, allowing 2 inches to extend over on each side. Lightly grease with oil.

Mix flour, powdered sugar, sifted cocoa, and butter well (or use food processor for 5–6 minutes or until it has the texture of a coarse meal).

Press mixture on bottom and sides of prepared pan, ¼ inch thick.

Bake crust at 350° F for 15 minutes.

Remove from oven. Sprinkle chocolate morsels on top; cool completely on a wire rack, about 30 minutes.

Whip together brown sugar, corn syrup, eggs, and melted butter until smooth. Stir in coconut and prepared pecans.

Spoon onto pie crust.

Bake 25–30 minutes, or until golden.

Cool at least 1 hour.

Lift from/remove from pan using foil. Cut into bars on a cutting board.

Printed in the USA
CPSIA information can be obtained
at www.ICGtesting.com
CBHW071758180724
11672CB00016B/349